WITHDRAWN
L. R. COLLEGE LIBRARY

enameling
for
beginners

ERRATUM

Page 23. Caption should read:

Decorative Accessories. Showing transparent green and ruby enamel fused to hand-hammered copper shapes. THE AUTHOR, 1961.

Page 64. Final line of lower caption should read:

Ash Tray, green, black and yellow. Painter's technique. RUTH DEUTSCH, 1958.

enameling
for
beginners

EDWARD WINTER

CARL A. RUDISILL LIBRARY
LENOIR RHYNE COLLEGE

watson-guptill publications
NEW YORK

To Robert A. Weaver,
Chairman of the Board, Ferro Corporation,
for his friendship, support,
and encouragement

738.4
W73e

55543
Sept. '66

Copyright 1962 by WATSON-GUPTILL PUBLICATIONS, INC., New York, N. Y.
Designed by BETTY BINS. All rights reserved.

Library of Congress Catalog Card Number: 61-15926

Printed in the United States by Civic Printing Co., Inc., New York, N. Y.

foreword

DURING THIRTY YEARS AS DIRECTING SUPERVISOR OF ART in the Cleveland Public Schools and Professor of Art at Western Reserve University, I have had ample opportunity to watch the phenomenal growth of the art of enameling. In spite of the wide interest it has inspired, the field is still relatively new to the student. Splendid opportunities are available to those willing to pursue a sound basic training offering the discipline necessary for working in the craft.

This book, which follows the author's highly successful *Enamel Art on Metals*, has grown from a desire to help the student and teacher understand the fundamental processes of enameling. These simplified instructions are the result of the author's experience as a teacher and pioneer in all of the new applications of enamel art.

Edward Winter has lived in Cleveland for many years and has participated there in the rapid rise of the craft of enameling both through the acclaim his work has received in many exhibitions in the United States and abroad and through his innovations in the fine art, industrial, and architectural uses of enamels. His efforts have placed him in the vanguard of his profession. The position that Cleveland now holds as a craft center second to none is due to the intensity with which the author and others have experimented in new, creative techniques.

Within the past four years the work of Edward Winter has been closely allied in the ecclesiastical field with that of his gifted wife, Thelma Frazier Winter. They have collaborated successfully on several church architectural projects, their newest commission being a six-hundred and thirty-four-square-foot enamel decoration for a Romanian Orthodox church in Cleveland. The warmth of feeling in this highly imaginative work strikes a refreshing note in an age so dominated by the machine.

By tradition we have assumed that enameling is an advanced craft and should not, therefore, be introduced before the secondary school level. In this book the author demonstrates that the enameling craft can be adapted to the needs of much younger students, opening up for them a new world of creative excitement. Basic training is thoroughly worked out through a series of easy, simplified techniques, dealing with the free expression of design, color, and texture, which will delight teachers and students alike.

The author's first book gave an impetus to enameling; numerous illustrations of Mr. Winter's work have helped to set a standard of creative potential and technical excellence that is hard to match. In the present book, further enriched by illustrations of Edward Winter's work, together with that of Thelma Frazier Winter, there is a systematic development of clear, step-by-step techniques in the use of enamels on copper, steel, and aluminum, with photographs of students actively engaged in making enamels. The future development of enameling in our schools and colleges will depend not only upon the knowledge of the teacher, who often is not able to devote adequate time to the mastery of the craft, but also upon the kind of leadership shown here.

We predict that *Enameling for Beginners* will enjoy a long, successful use. The freshness of viewpoint, systematic control, sound craftsmanship, and high degree of taste shown by Edward Winter should go far to inspire the student in the craft of enameling.

ALFRED HOWELL
Former Directing Supervisor of Art
Cleveland Public Schools

contents

Acknowledgements

I should like to express my appreciation to several people without whose cooperation this book would not have been nearly so effective: my wife, Thelma Frazier Winter, for several of her fine, imaginative enamels reproduced here; Art Supervisor A. G. Pelikan; artist-educator Alfred Howell for his kind words about the author; Mrs. Roy Tait for the tile drawings, and her children, Jackie and David, for their work on stencils; Linda Vantaggi for the step-by-step processes of making an ash tray; the six students making jewelry under the direction of Donald Larson, Custer High School, Milwaukee, Wisconsin; Mrs. Edith Sims and students of Chestnut School, North Olmsted, Ohio; Michael Cushnier for his enamels on driftwood, instructor Carla Zawacki, Best School, Oak Park, Illinois; Pauline Johnson for her three-dimensional paper forms from her book *Creating with Paper*; George Rickey for his clever "Dyptich"; Patricia Easterbrook Roberts for her metal flowers from *How to Make Flower Arrangements*; Thomas Hardy for his iron "Bison"; Obediah Fisher of East Technical High School, Cleveland, for his "Painted Enamels" mounted on wood; Henry Karg of Ferro Corporation for his contribution featured in the step-by-step photographs in Enameling Steel and Aluminum; Stephanie Kochmann for her portrait of a girl, teacher and supervisor Charles B. Jeffrey, Shaker High School, Shaker Heights, Ohio; Sharleen Burket and Kenneth Tolarella for their silk screen enameling, with teacher Arthur Cipollo of Collinwood High School, Cleveland, and supervisor Ronald Day; Howard Fox of Collinwood and Robert Novak of St. Edward's School, Cleveland, for their silk screen design under instructor Norman Magden.

The photographs are by Dwight Boyer, Oliver Baker, and Richard and Blanche Godfrey of the Cleveland Museum of Art; Marion Gregor, Robert Hoffner, Whitie Martin, Donald Normark, Irving Hartley, Martin Linsey, Parade Studios, William Wynne, and the author.

introduction

IN THIS BOOK, which is a companion to my first work, *Enamel Art on Metals*, I have made an effort to repeat little of the previous material and have concentrated instead upon basic application processes and new techniques. While some of the text and technical terms may seem at first rather complicated for the beginner, the accompanying photographs will clarify all processes for the student, regardless of his age level.

It is an accepted fact that no other art-craft has enjoyed such rapid growth and success in the short span of thirty years. Today, both enamels and metals have experienced revolutionary changes, and their production is an exacting science. The enamelist can take advantage of this progress and use it to attain greater technical perfection in his own work. Even the ingredients of enamel mixtures can be adjusted to apply to all types of metals—copper, steel, cast iron, and aluminum.

Having access for over thirty years to the modern development laboratories of the Ferro Corporation in Cleveland, Ohio has enabled me to observe the phenomenal potentialities of metal enameling. Teachers and professional craftsmen can profit from a knowledge of these new methods as they are explained at the student level. Teachers who develop thoughtful and creative attitudes in their students are aware of the ease and spontaneity with which children use the popular media, poster paint, crayons, and chalk. It is my hope that vitreous enamel will lend itself to the same simplified handling, since the liquid wet ground "slush" enamels have the same consistency as poster paint and are thinned by adding water. In addition, the sieve application method I learned at the Kunstgewerbeschule of Vienna has given the art of enameling an added freedom by permitting large areas of metal to be covered successfully. Liquid opaque or transparent enamels can be applied to flat or three-dimensional objects through dipping or spraying.

It is exciting to imagine a class of eager students working on projects that will be durable and attractive works of art. In order to obtain the best efforts of the student, we know that the teacher must integrate materials, tools, techniques, and aesthetics. It is my aim in this book to help the teacher do this. I hope, in addition, that the students, craft counselors, amateurs, hobbyists, and top professional artists and designers will find the work presented here of value in their exploration into the creative world of metals.

elements

earth and fire

I INVITE THE READER to think of a large number of things that make life more pleasant and convenient for all of us.

You prepared for today in a bathroom with gleaming porcelain walls and fixtures and a tile floor. You ate your breakfast from China dishes and drank from a glass. The food had been cooked on an enameled stove, possibly in enameled steel cooking utensils. Your light for reading comes through glass windows or from lamps enclosed in glass. Insulators carry the wires bringing electricity into home or school. Firebrick lines the school heating furnace. Sewer pipe and drain tile carry away waste water, and enameled signs label various rooms. Further reciting of names of all the items of this sort that surround you is not necessary. You can think of dozens of them: bottles, jars, flower pots, chimneys, and what not. And every bit of the metal anywhere had its start in a furnace or kiln built of firebrick.

All of these things are made of earth and fire. Ceramics is the subject that deals with making them, and the science that finds out how to do it in the best way. Enameling of metals is one of the most important branches of ceramics.

All young people should know about the ceramic industries which operate on earthy raw materials by fire or heat, and about the sands, clays, and other earths that are dug out of the ground to make up the materials for ceramic products. In describing the composi-

The blasted feldspar and silica ore is removed from the pit and placed in giant crushers, which reduce the particles to a size small enough to be ground to fine dust in a ball mill. The 200 or 270 mesh particles undergo rigid quality checks before being sold to the ceramic and enameling industry.

1

The foothills of the Walapai Mountains in northwestern Arizona have been for the past twenty seven years a large source of feldspar and silica for the enameling industry. It is estimated that an additional thirty years supply of ore can be blasted from this pit.

Photos, courtesy International Minerals & Chemicals, Skokie, Ill.

tion of these earthy substances, we occasionally enter the field of chemistry.

In the same way we must say something about fire and what happens when fuel burns, and how to confine the heat from blazing fuels in kilns and furnaces to do the work of ceramics.

Many people used to think of "ceramics" as meaning vases and jars on the shelves of museums or fragments of pottery found in the ruins of ancient cities. Those pieces serve to illustrate, as lasting relics, the degrees of culture and of artistic advancement of the older cvilizations.

Today, nearly everyone knows, or should know, that ceramics includes a large number and great variety of industries and products, taking in everything that can be done with earth and fire.

Some of the earths that are used in ceramics can be scooped up or shoveled from beds of the material (as illustrated). Others are made by crushing rocks such as limestone or sandstones. A few are obtained from chemicals manufactured from such substances as common salt. The sand used by glassmakers is so clean and pure that nothing can grow in it.

Many years ago when men wrote all their scientific books in Latin, one of the natural philosophers declared, *"Sine igne, nihil operamur."* This meant, and still means to us, that without fire we can do nothing. We need fire to cook our food, to warm our homes, to make power, to get metals from ores, and to produce by heat thousands of things that we use.

Excerpted from *Earth and Fire* by Samuel R. Scholes, Ph.D., Sc.D., Emeritus Professor of Glass Technology, State University of New York, College of Ceramics, Alfred, New York.

2

These raw materials for opaque white enamels will melt into liquid glass in from three and a half to four hours smelting at 2300°F. By changing the proportions of the ingredients, the opacity or transparency, hardness or softness of enamel is determined.

ARSENIC OXIDE

POTASSIUM CARBONATE

SILICA

from raw materials to liquid enamels

BORAX

LEAD OXIDE

Jet flames are directed onto the enamel to keep it flowing freely. The molten enamel can either be poured into tanks of water to break it up into small particles called "frit" or poured onto heavy steel slabs to cool before it is broken up into large lumps with a hammer or crusher.

3

The enamel is wet ground in this ball mill. A typical mixture for this small size mill would be 100 parts of frit, 6 parts of clear clay, ¼ part of potassium carbonate, and 40 cubic centimeters (about one cup) of water. This produces a "slip" or "slush" enamel.

This Bacilla ball mill, which is ideal for school use, is equipped with a 1/6 H.P., 115 volt motor.

4

RIGHT: *Small or large lumps of frit can be crushed into powder that will pass through an 80 or 100 mesh sieve. Place the lumps in the mortar and strike a few blows with the hammer. The powder is then shaken through a sieve onto clean paper, ready to be used for dry process application.*

The slip or slush enamel is now ready for use and can be stored in glass jars or plastic bags. The bags are ideal for school use, as they are less dangerous to handle. Enamel in this form is applied by dipping or spraying.

When grinding is completed, the enamel is dumped, along with the porcelain grinding balls, into a large 200 mesh brass sieve resting on a basin. The slush enamel is then shaken through the sieve into the basin.

Opaque white enamel in three forms: frit lump, 80 mesh, and 200 mesh.

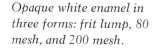

tools
and
materials

ENAMELING TOOLS

From left to right: emery cloth, rubbing stone or carborundum, table vice, steel stake, tinning shears, planishing hammer, and file. Other metal working tools can be added as the student progresses.

FURNACE FORKS

Chromel steel tongs and fork can be used for placing enamel pieces in and out of the furnace.

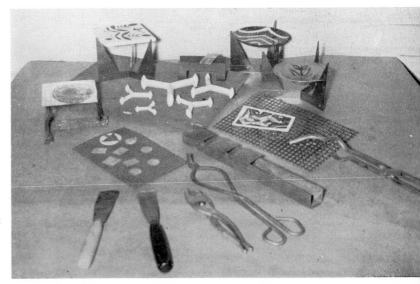

FIRING SUPPORTS
Chromel steel trivets, fire-clay stilts, and chromel wire screens support enamel pieces for firing. Enamels of unusual shape may need specially designed trivets to hold them successfully.

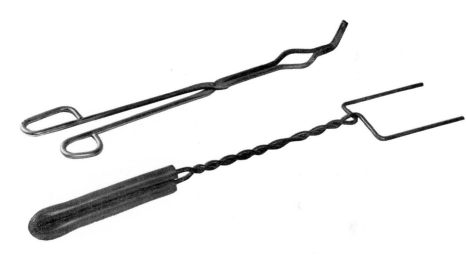

GUM TRAGACANTH
Gum tragacanth, a whitish vegetable gum derived from sea plants, is applied in solution form to metal surfaces to bind the dry, sifted enamel upon them before firing. The flakes should be dissolved by boiling in a basin of water. The resultant solution, which should have a watery consistency, is applied with a camel's hair brush. A few drops of alcohol will keep it from fermenting. Gum tragacanth can be purchased at most drug stores.

enamel

ENAMEL IS A LOW TEMPERATURE GLASS compounded so that it may be fused successfully onto the surfaces of metals such as copper, steel, cast iron, silver, and aluminum. This vitreous enamel is produced in transparent, opaque, and semi-opaque forms. When applying and fusing the *transparent* enamel on copper, the surface of the copper shows through; the *opaque* variety completely covers and hides the metal; while the *semi-opaque* or *opalescent* type allows the surface metal to show through in a slightly clouded manner. Unlike the stained glass of church windows, which allows the light to pass through, transparent enamels fired over a polished metal surface give off a reflective light from the metal itself, which is luminous, deep-toned, and vibrant.

Enamels have been used ever since early man learned to melt colored glass onto copper to produce jewelry, to ornament pottery, and to decorate objects made of glass. However, traditional techniques, discussed in my earlier book, *Enamel Art on Metals*, will not be dealt with here. The aim of this book is simply to describe and illustrate processes of application and technique never before described, since they are the product of the author's study and experimentation through years of work with the medium. However, before proceeding further, it should be made clear that there is no similarity between the paint called "enamel," which has a glossy surface, and our vitreous enamel, which is glass. In order to make this distinction clear, the manufacturers of vitreous enamels some-

8

times refer to their product as "glass" or "porcelain" enamel. Our reference in this book will be to "vitreous enamels" and their application to various metals, which will be described in later chapters.

The manufacture of enamels and enamel frit

The enamels which are available to us today are the products of technical research and development, which have not only perfected the basic material, but have given us an almost unlimited number of colors from which to choose. Although it is important for the student to know the raw materials from which enamels are made and the methods of manufacture, he will probably never be called upon to make his own. Vitreous enamel is the product of the melting together of the correct proportion of materials* (shown in previous photographs) in a smelter which reaches a temperature of approximately 2100°F. It is a fascinating experience to stand before the huge smelter and watch the white-hot molten glass, which looks very much like strings of taffy, being poured out to cool on large steel slabs. As it strikes the comparatively cool metal, it becomes hardened and thick. It is then broken into pieces by a sledge hammer and put into suitable containers to await further grinding into finer particles for final use. Another way in which enamel is produced is by allowing the stream of molten glass to pour between two revolving steel rollers to produce a flake form, which breaks up into smaller pieces. In still another method, the molten glass is poured into a tank of water, which breaks it into small particles. In all cases, these small enamel particles are called "frit."

The enamelist may order from the supplier small quantities of large and small lumps as they are first broken up, but the more finely ground frit is customarily and most easily used. The frit is processed by crushing and grinding and then separated into quantities having uniform particles by the use of various size sieves, which are referred to by the number of openings per square inch in the screen, such as 60, 80, 100, or 200 mesh. Thus, the size of the frit particles in a 60 mesh grind is much larger than those of 80 or 100 mesh; while frit of 200 mesh has been reduced to almost powder form. The 80 mesh grind, which has a slightly finer appearance than

* Refer to Traditional Techniques as explained in the author's previous book *Enamel Art on Metals*.

table salt, is considered the most satisfactory for the ordinary uses of the enameler.

Since we have briefly described the process of smelting and grinding frit, we may also define the term "flux." Flux is a transparent enamel of the same composition and grind as the enamel just described. Many transparent colors, such as ruby, purple, yellow, pink, light blue, and some greens, are more brilliant and beautiful when they are fired over a previously fired layer of clear flux. A hard firing flux is used for this purpose, and a soft, easier flowing flux may be used as a surface upon which to apply small flat wires known as cloissons. When the flux melts, the wires sink into it and are held in place upon cooling, forming a wire design which can then be filled with various colored enamels to make a cloissoné design.

Another form of enamel is known as "slush" or "slip" enamel. It is a creamy liquid which may be applied to metals by dipping or spraying. It can produce decorative and exciting results, one of which is an interesting crackle or tearing effect.

While it is much easier to order enamel already ground to the consistency desired, there are a few colors, such as the greens and light blues, which have a tendency to absorb moisture and chemicals from the air much more quickly than the others when finely ground. If not used within two to three weeks, they fire out in a slightly cloudy surface when applied directly to copper. If the weather is extremely damp and the enamels are not kept in a tightly capped jar, they may be affected sooner. Other colors, such as the transparent browns and dark blue, seem to be least affected through long storage periods. The traditional jewelers and enamelers knew of this danger and kept small portions of ground enamel in porcelain containers. When they finished working, they would cover the enamel with water and place a lid over it to keep it free from dust or dirt in the air. Quart-size Mason jars with rubber rings provide good containers in which to keep enamels not in use.

Color in enamels

A complete book could be written about the science of producing colors and the great assortment of subtle tones and shades which are crafted. With most manufacturers, these formulae are closely guarded secrets and are usually handed down from father to son. Color is given to the glass enamels by the addition of certain metallic oxides before the raw material batch is smelted, and during this melting process the colored enamel is made.

This pertains to the transparent, opaque, and opalescent varieties. Liquid slush or enamel slip colors are processed differently, since colorants and oxides are added to the clear enamel frit by the manufacturer and ground up with the addition of prescribed proportions of water, fine clay, and chemical salts in a porcelain ball mill. With the many available metallic oxides and their varied combinations and percentages, one can readily see that in both coloring systems many hundreds of colors and values are possible. This gives the enamelist an extremely wide color range in which to work. If you wish to attempt to make a new color out of those which you have on hand, you will find that 80 mesh enamels are not finely enough ground to intermix successfully. When enamel is ground to 150 or 200 mesh, various shades of orange can be made by mixing opaque red with opaque lemon yellow. A light blue mixed with ruby will produce, according to the proportions used, a red or blue lavender.

Types of enamels

Each metal—copper, steel, silver or aluminum—has its own particular type of enamel which has been compounded individually for maximum fusion. Enamels for steel, copper, and silver are similar in so far as firing temperature is concerned, fusing after two to three minutes at 1450 to 1500°F. However, for aluminum, which itself will melt at slightly over 1200°F., enamels which fuse at 1000°F. have been specially compounded by ceramic engineers. After years of research, satisfactory enamels for aluminum have been produced. These lower firing enamels are not interchangeable with the types designed for the harder metals and any attempt to use them on the other metals will prove disappointing. If steel or cast iron has a coating of fired opaque enamel, one can then apply transparent copper or silver enamels on top satisfactorily.

Of all the metals and enamels available for use, I have found that enamel on copper is still the most rewarding in regard to color, quality of surface, transparency, texture, and design possibilities. However, when one considers the wide assortment of metals, enamels, and colors available to the teacher, the student, and the professional artist, one must marvel at the great prospects for future use and exploitation.

copper

COPPER IS THE METAL perhaps most commonly used by the enameler. Relatively soft in comparison to steel, ductile and malleable, it is very satisfactory for work which requires stretching by hammering and bending. Transparent enamels can be fired directly upon it to produce colors of depth and luminosity. This richness is the result of the sheen of the polished copper surface appearing through the fired enamel. When 18 gauge copper is hammered and planished, virtually every hammer mark will give off an assortment of reflected light and color effects.

Copper is most commonly available in sheet or roll form. The sheets measure 30 inches by 60 inches or 20 inches by 90 inches, while rolls may be bought in six, eight, ten, twelve, fourteen, and sixteen inch widths. Copper can also be purchased from the supplier in various size tubes suitable for making tall vase forms. One metal manufacturer also sells small sheets of copper with unusual embossed designs, such as radiating lines, star shapes, and cross-hatching, many of which are machine engraved or die stamped.

Only pure copper can be enameled successfully, so it is important when ordering it to ask for "electrolytic, cold-rolled, annealed" stock. Never allow anyone to sell you roofing copper, which is an alloy containing certain amounts of zinc and other metals. When this metal is subjected to the intense heat required in enameling, cracks and blisters will appear in the fired enamel upon the second firing. Since most enameled pieces, before they are completed, must be fired three or four times, you can see that this impure metal would not be satisfactory. Often the question of enameling brass or bronze arises. These yellow metals are also alloys. Brass is composed of one-third zinc, which makes it extremely difficult to enamel because, on cooling, the enamel will pop off. Bronze, which is composed of ninety per cent copper and ten per cent tin, is unpredictable and difficult as well, but on a heavy cast form, it can be used for name plates and monumental tables, if a low temperature opaque enamel is used.

However, there is one alloy, a wonderful, reddish copper called "tonbac," which our enamel class used when I was a student in Vienna. It was a specially smelted copper containing a small amount of zinc. While we do not have this exact type of metal in this country, the one which compares most closely to it, I have discovered, is "guilder's metal." It contains ninety-five per cent copper and five per cent zinc and can be used for firing transparent ruby red enamel directly on the surface, without first applying an undercoat of flux to the metal. When firing ruby red over regular copper, transparent flux must first be used for successful results. This will be further considered in the chapter Enameling Copper.

The thickness of copper is determined by the Brown & Sharp gauge, which is a system of numbers ranging from 0000 to 40, each indicating a definite thickness in thousandths of an inch. The larger the gauge number, the thinner the metal. A "number 14 gauge" sheet is about one-sixteenth of an inch thick. One should work with at least an 18 gauge copper, since this heavy weight produces the best work. For the beginner as well as the professional, a number of firings is usually necessary to complete the piece; heavy copper will best stand up under these several firings. The thinner gauge copper such as 20-22 or 24 can be enameled successfully, but it requires greater skill and experience to obtain the desired results. There are many commercial, die-stamped, and spun copper shapes on the market. Most of them are bad in proportion, shape, and design, but the greatest disadvantage is that they are produced from copper that is too thin for successful enameling. The intense heat of the furnace is too much for the thin metal, and several successive firings will be injurious to the piece. Objects made from heavy copper have the feeling of weight and quality which adds greatly to their value and appreciation by the public.

I am sure that craft classes in many schools have been working with copper for a long time, and students have learned the ease and fun of working with it. Now they can experience the added thrill of applying and firing vitreous enamels to it.

enameling copper

COPPER CAN BE SUCCESSFULLY ENAMELED in several ways: by dry process application through a sieve, by dipping the metal into a basin of liquid slush or slip enamel, or by spraying. There is a reason for using each method, for the final surfaces of the objects will vary in each of these techniques.

The traditional enamelers used a steel spatula or pointer to apply the ground enamel in wet form (grain by grain) to the copper. This method was painstaking and produced stilted results. Large surfaces of the metal could never be covered in this manner. In the course of teaching the first class of enameling to be offered in this country, I was able to introduce to my students the easier and faster application method of sifting the 80 mesh enamel powder onto the metal by use of a large sieve. The sieve, which is about five inches in diameter, can be easily held and manipulated with the hand. The screen opening of 80 mesh per square inch allows the 80 mesh enamel to fall through by the gentle shaking of the wrist. Both opaque and transparent enamels can be applied to copper by use of the sifting operation, but the most highly transparent enamel colored surfaces can be obtained only by the dry application. With this method, the surface of the copper must first be coated with a thin solution of gum tragacanth (explained in another section of this book), which acts as a light adhesive to hold the powdered

14

enamel onto the metal until it is fired. The enamel supplier can furnish transparent enamels milled up in alcohol for dipping or spraying, but the colors when fired are rather thin and weak looking. Only with the dry process application can the real depth of jewel-like surface quality be achieved.

Copper can also be enameled with opaque enamels by dipping or spraying. The supplier can furnish all colors as well as black and white. This enamel is prepared by grinding clear clay and inorganic salts together in a porcelain ball mill for three or four hours. The inorganic salts act as a suspending agent which keeps the slush or slip enamel in a creamy state. This enamel, used for dipping and spraying, must be ground fine enough to pass through a 200 to 250 mesh screen.

Accompanying photographs illustrating the dipping of copper animals into the enamel slip show graphically the ease and advantage of this application process.

Finely ground enamels can also be applied to copper by spraying with a hand container called Jet-Pak (illustrated in another section). A harmless gas propellant in the can produces the pressure necessary to spray the enamel that is placed in the glass cup attachment.

If larger spray equipment is desired, the usual compressor and air gun or air brush is used. This necessitates at least thirty-five to forty pounds air pressure.

Copper is my favorite metal, for when handled with care and respect, it responds accordingly. In using transparent enamels on copper, one can produce bowls, plaques, and murals of great quality and technical excellence. In keeping a record of my enamel works in museums throughout the world, I have found that the majority are on copper.

Many persons, both young and old, have a tendency to shift from one metal to another; they want to acquire the tricks and unusual effects before they have developed a technical mastery or skill in working with copper. Each metal that can be enameled has its own distinct characteristics, and a craftsman could easily devote a lifetime to any one of them without exhausting its decorative and utilitarian potentialities.

A suitable ash tray, about three and one half inches in diameter, is made by using a pencil and compass or a disc on 18 gauge copper.

making an enamel ash tray

Shears are used to cut out the copper circle.

Using a rawhide mallet, the copper disc is hammered over a rounded iron stake to form a shallow tray.

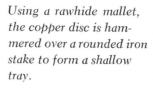

The tray is placed on the edge of a work bench so that the tray's edge can be smoothed with a flat-edge, medium size file.

After the piece has been cleaned with steel wool, scouring powder, and water, it is rinsed clean (an acid bath can be dispensed with if the piece is sufficiently clean). A large camel's hair brush is used to coat the metal with a watery solution of gum tragacanth.

The 80 mesh black enamel is sifted onto the wet coated metal surface through an 80 mesh sieve. A large paper placed underneath catches the enamel.

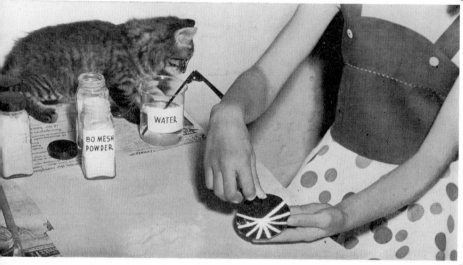

To dampen the black enamel powder, a light spray of water is applied with the mouth blower. The powder applied with the fingers will then adhere to the black enamel surface.

Another light spray of water will dampen the white stripes.

A hot plate dries the piece before it is placed in the furnace.
A wire screen and small metal tripods hold the tray while it is drying.

When firing enamels, be sure to wear asbestos or finger gloves and to use long crucible tongs to place the wire screen and tray in the furnace. An interval timer clock (set for two and one half minutes) may be used.

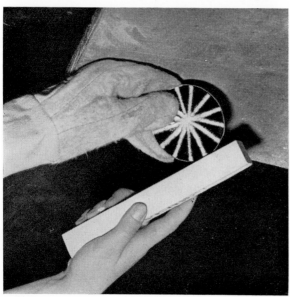

A carborundum stone or emery cloth is used to smooth the edge of the piece. For further polishing use a cotton buffing wheel with rouge compound. Clear, hard lacquer applied with a brush protects the polished edge.

These accessories designed by the author show how effective white stripes are on a black background.

making an enamel bowl

To make a bowl, the copper disc is placed in a cup-shaped hollow in the top of a hardwood log. The copper is shaped into a deep-sided bowl by gradually turning the disc with one hand while striking it with a rounded stake held in the other.

After the bowl has been raised to the depth desired, it is turned upside down over a polished round stake held securely in a vice. A slightly rounded planishing hammer evens the surface of the metal, at the same time producing a surface of hammer marks that will be visible through transparent fired enamel.

A one-quarter horsepower motor with an emery-rubber wheel, available at most hardware stores, can be used to smooth the edges of the metal.

After the bowl has been cleaned with scouring powder, water, and fine steel wool, then rinsed in clean water, it is ready to be coated with a thin solution of gum tragacanth, using a camel's hair brush.

Hold the bowl on the bottom side, shaking the 80 mesh ground enamel onto it through a large 80 mesh sieve. Using a mouth blower, spray clear water lightly onto the surface of the piece, being careful that the enamel does not run down the sides. After the bowl has thoroughly dried over a hot plate, it is ready to be fired.

other

simple

projects

A young student is proud of his decorated wood plaque, made with enameled copper squares cemented to the top of large, flat-headed nails.

Students are fascinated by enamel fusing in the heat of the furnace and wait eagerly for the teacher to remove the pieces.

Six young enamelers working on classroom projects.

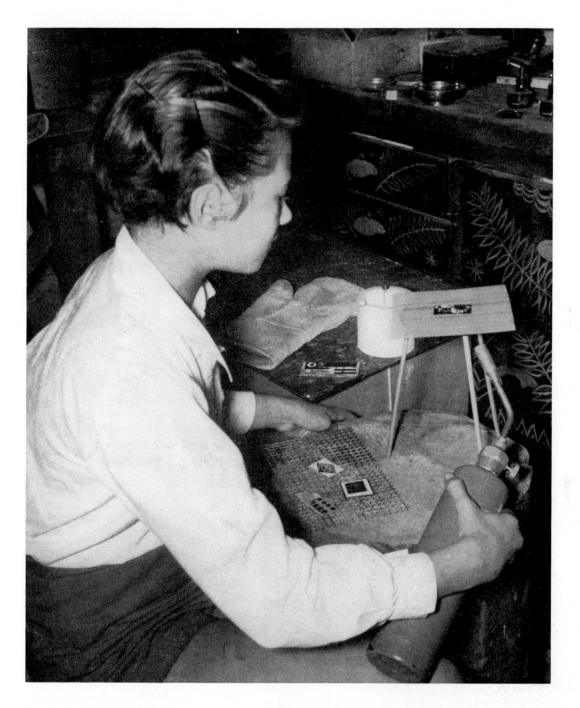

A furnace is not needed to fuse enamel to small pieces of metal. This student is using a Bernz-o-matic hand torch equipped with a cylinder of refrigerant gas (replaceable at any hardware store). Instructions for use come with each burner. The small enamel rests on a chromel (heat resisting) metal screen, while the flame is directed onto the piece from the underside of the tripod.

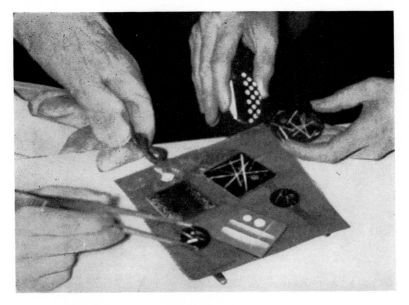

Opaque enamel thread and colorful lumps of frit decorate these small pieces. Concentrated gum tragacanth solution adheres enamel textures to surfaces that have been previously fired.

Two students coat their copper ash trays with a solution of gum tragacanth preparatory to applying the enamel.

from
cut paper
to enameled
metal

BEFORE THE STUDENT ATTEMPTS TO CUT and bend sheet copper into three-dimensional forms, he should experiment with paper.

Paper is cheap and plentiful, easy to bend and fold, and already has enjoyed wide usage, from elementary through college levels. Paper is an inspiring material and a challenge to the imagination. It has found such eager acceptance that there are already several good books available on paper folding and modeling. *Creating with Paper*, by Pauline Johnson, of the School of Art, University of Washington, Seattle, is one of the best. I recommend this informative book with its exciting illustrations to all enamelers, as it serves to stimulate thinking in three-dimensional terms. A few examples are shown in this book.

There are many different types of paper, each with its own characteristics arising from organic structure. Papers have textures, tensile strength, and varying degrees of opacity—they can be rough, smooth, transparent, opaque, thin or thick. With several types of paper at hand, the student learns which holds its shape and works best. Bristle-board paper and photographers' print paper (which can be dampened to hold a shape) are popular. The bird cutouts in the accompanying photographs were made from manila tablet paper. Transparent scotch tape held the birds together on a wire coat hanger framework.

Heavy cardboard must be used for the rigid vertical or horizontal planes necessary to make a stabile structure stand by itself.

An abstract sculptural effect can be achieved by vertical planes with horizontal inserts attached by slits in the cardboard, as shown in one of the accompanying reproductions.

27

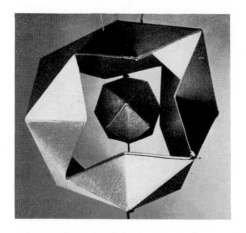

This cardboard polyhedron is made with two cut, squared sections fitted together. A similar three-dimensional piece could be made in enameled metal.

paper animals
and forms

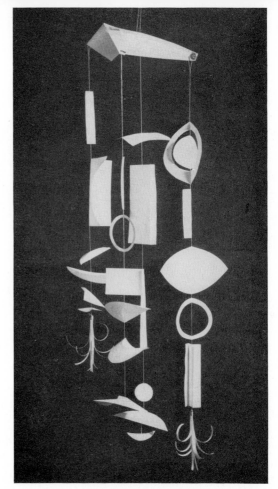

ABOVE RIGHT: *Unusual effects of shape and movement are produced by using suspended forms of paper or cardboard attached with threads. Similar shapes can be made with enamels and piano wire.*

Cardboard construction showing interlocking open planes that relate successfully to one another. This type of construction would be most successful in enameled metal.

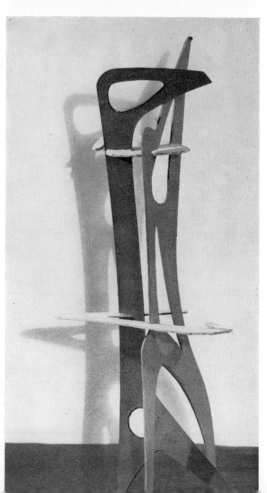

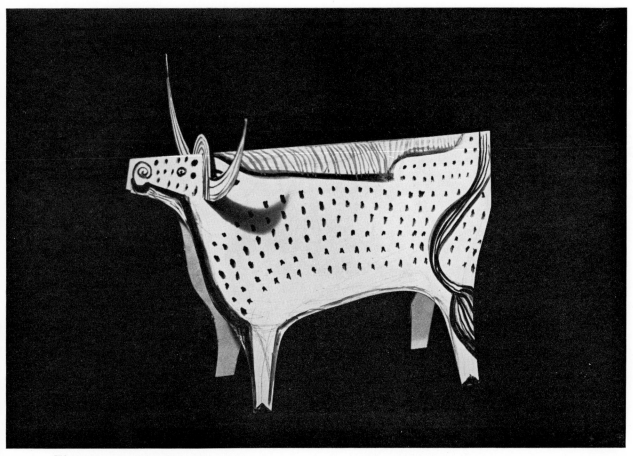

This paper cow is made with a center division for easy standing. Black crayon was used for realistic surface detail.

A somber hippo makes an interesting cut paper shape.

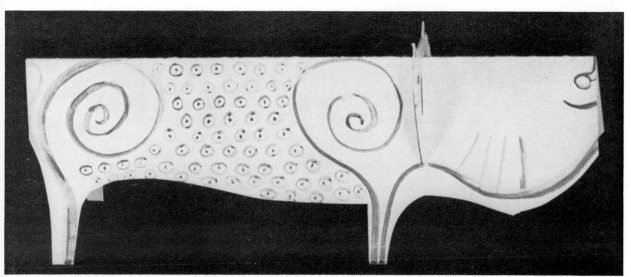

This amusing lion is a cardboard and crayon creation.

Construction paper, tape, cement, and staples made this cylindrical fowl.

Using scissors and medium weight manila paper, complicated birds can be created. Onto a framework of bent wire, the bodies, wings, and heads of the rooster and other birds can be applied with transparent tape. A wad of modeling clay can be used as a temporary base to support the wire armature.

30

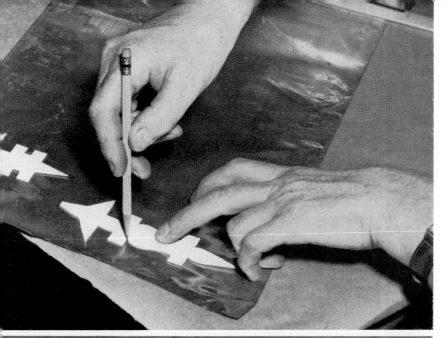

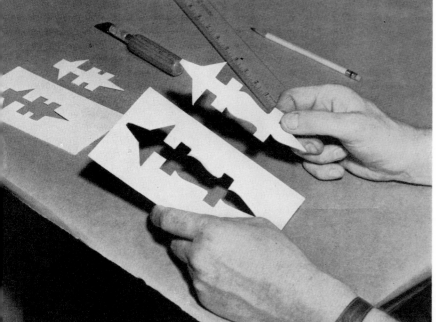

making
copper
animals

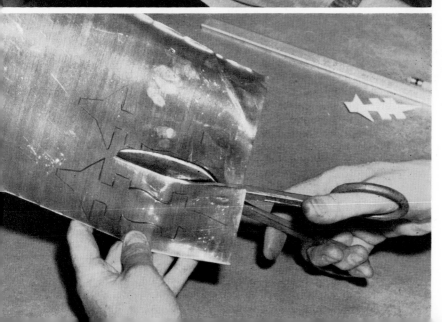

TOP: *The flat patterns of the dogs shown here are first drawn on thin cardboard and then cut out with a stencil knife or mat-cutting knife.*

CENTER: *Next, the paper pattern is placed on the 22 gauge copper and traced around with a pencil.*

BOTTOM: *Tinning shears cut the copper along the pencil lines. Later, the piece of metal should be placed on a flat surface and scrubbed with cleansing powder and a stiff brush or steel wool.*

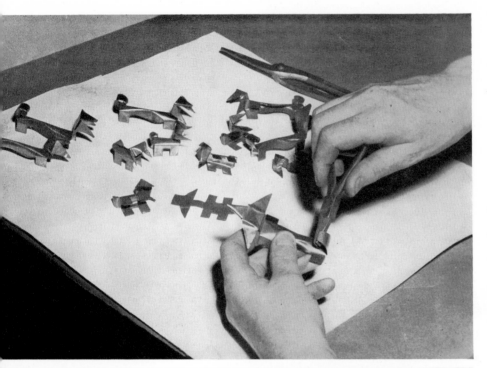

After the copper has been scrubbed to a high brightness, the worker's hands should be washed to prevent getting grease or perspiration marks on the metal. With round nosed pliers, the legs, tail, and ears of the animal can be bent into the proper position.

Then, held by the edge of the tail, the animal can be dipped into a basin of slush or slip opaque enamel. After two or three brisk shakes with the wrist to remove excess enamel, it can be placed on a hot plate to dry.

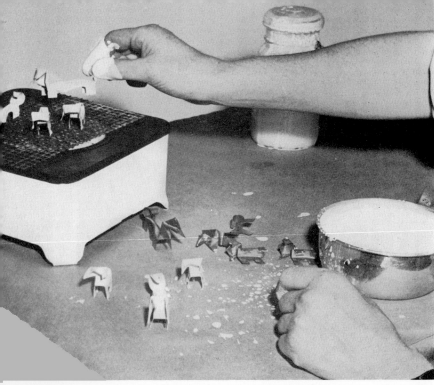

Fifteen or twenty minutes is enough to dry the enamel thoroughly. The opposite end of a brush dipped into black enamel is an effective tool for making the dog's eyes.

The dogs may be fired individually or several at a time, using a chromel wire screen. Two and a half minutes at 1500°F. is sufficient to fuse the enamel.

When completed, the
black and white dogs can
be used in many ways to
create interesting arrangements.

An assortment of amusing animals can be created with
glistening, fired enamel. BY THE AUTHOR, 1935

BISON *Executed in sheet iron with the use of a welding torch. An ideal surface for a protective coating of enamel.* THOMAS HARDY, Courtesy Kraushaar Gallery, New York

other forms from metal

THE SEASONS *This piece is not enameled but constructed of steel polychrome sheets applied to a wire framework.* GEORGE RICKEY, Courtesy Kraushaar Gallery, New York

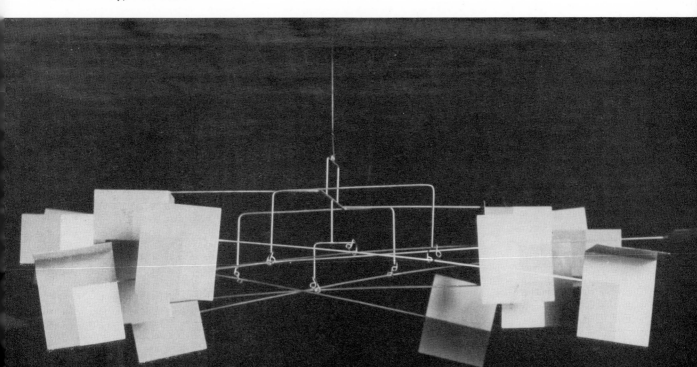

APRIL SHOWERS *A gay enamel on copper. The umbrella and lips are bright opaque red; the hat, collar, and cuffs are light blue.* THELMA AND EDWARD WINTER, *1938*

This fireside bouquet of flowers made from 22 gauge copper presents a potential for enameling in assorted colors. PATRICIA EASTERBROOK ROBERTS, Courtesy Viking Press, New York

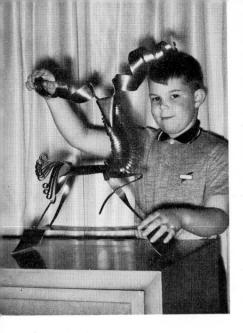

FAR LEFT: A young student examines this metal deer made by a craftsman in Vienna in 1929. The animal was cut from one piece of sheet metal. Such a piece would lend itself to enameling.

LEFT: By brazing bolts to the back side of the copper cut outs before they are enameled, the finished pieces can be used as colorful wall decorations.

These fishes, turtles, shells, and flowers were made from 18 gauge copper. Turquoise transparent enamel was fired over an opaque white surface. Red and white accents were also used. BY THE AUTHOR, 1958

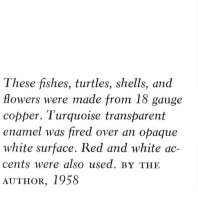

The colorful, stylized birds harmonize with the turquoise mosaic over the doors and base of the pool. Main entrance to the cafeteria building, Columbus State School, Columbus, Ohio, 1958

OPHELIA   *This cylindrical decorative piece was made from 18 gauge copper. The flower as well as the disc have turquoise transparent enamel fused over silver foil.*
THELMA AND EDWARD WINTER, *1938*

steel

SHEET STEEL is not as easy to shape and form by hand as the more malleable metals such as copper or silver, but it can be spun and die stamped into almost any shape desired. Enameled steel has an advantage over other metals: it can withstand greater shock and impact before chipping or cracking. Also, it is the cheapest of all metals in both large and small quantities. Extremely fine enameling steel of low carbon variety has been perfected over a period of many years by steel producing companies. Called "enameling stock," it can be purchased from the suppliers listed under Materials and Supplies in the back of this book.

Preparing and cleaning

While it is possible, with proper acid cleaning, to enamel regular carbon steel in the form of sheets, tubes, rods or wire, it is best to use the regular enameling stock made specifically for enamels. The light gray surface of this steel is usually covered with an oil film as protection against rust, but with fine steel wool, a stiff brush, and kitchen scouring powder and brisk rubbing, the metal surface can be made clean enough for enameling. In factories, where uniform production runs are necessary, the steel passes through a hot alkali cleaning solution, is then rinsed in clean water and later subjected to a hot sulphuric acid and water pickle. Six per cent acid is used, which slightly etches the steel when it is immersed for twenty or thirty minutes.

Pieces of steel that are cleaned and set aside for enameling a few days later may begin to show small rust spots within twenty-four to ninety-eight hours; so the student must be warned to enamel the metal shortly after it has been cleaned. Pieces of steel can be kept clean and free from rusting for days, however, providing they are first placed in a neutralizing solution of ninety per cent soda ash, ten per cent borax, and warm water. After a twenty minute period in this solution, the pieces of steel should be wiped dry, wrapped in clean paper, and stored in a warm place.

Silver-plated steel may also be enameled successfully. There are suppliers of small steel shapes with silver-plated surfaces upon which transparent enamels can be fused. Greater care must be given to firing this steel, for too many insertions into the hot furnace may spoil and dull the colors. However, a few experimental tests will enable the student to produce the best possible results by learning its limitations and potentials.

Aluminum-plated steel called "aluminized steel" is also available. Regular aluminum enamels are used (see following section) and fired at 1000°F. for a ten minute period.

Stainless steel can be enameled with regular steel enamels, provided the metal is first roughened slightly by sand blasting with air pressure. The bright stainless steel surface is so wonderful in itself that for the most effective results a design might be enameled, leaving some areas of the bright metal surface showing.

It does not require too much imagination for the artist to realize the full potential of sheet steel as a base metal for enameling.

enameling steel

STEEL HAS BEEN ENAMELED commercially for more than fifty years. The earliest enameling of this metal was done in Germany, but the methods and formulae of the enamels used were brought to the United States many years ago. Today this is one of our greatest industries. It was discovered by the early enamelers that a preliminary enamel coat of high cobalt and iron content (dark blue), known in the industry as "ground coat," was best for firing onto the steel surface. Once the ground coat has been fired onto the metal, it serves as a fine base for further application of white, black, and colored enamels.

Steel can be enameled by dipping or spraying. Both processes, as the accompanying step-by-step photos illustrate, are simple. Into a basin three-quarters filled with the blue ground coat enamel, the piece of steel that is to be enameled (held on the edges by the fingers) is dipped. The excess enamel can be shaken off by a sharp jerking motion of the hands. The piece can then be placed upon a nail board to dry. The dipping process covers the front and back sides of the metal at the same time, thus solving the usually difficult counter enameling problem.

When the ground coat has completely dried onto the steel, it is ready to be fired at 1500 to 1520°F. for a period of three minutes. Some low temperature ground coats which fuse at 1400° and less are now available. The tendency during the past few years has been to fire enamels upon steel at lower temperatures, which also prevents any warping of the metal.

Ground coat enamel can be sprayed onto the metal with spray gun and compressor equipment. Forty-pound air pressure is necessary for successful spraying of the enamel. If a ground coat is ground longer in a ball mill and becomes extremely fine, it can be sprayed with less air pressure and used successfully in a small air brush. In spraying, all sides of the metal can be completely covered with enamel by drying one side before the opposite one is sprayed.

Within the past three years, several steel companies have developed a pure steel that permits specially compounded white enamels to be fused directly onto the surface without the need of blue ground coat. One company calls this metal "Univite," while another lists theirs as "Bethnamel." The opaque white enamels are fused onto these special steels at from 1440 to 1500°F. After an opaque enamel is fused onto steel, one can apply any of the regular transparent enamels to this surface and fuse them successfully. Transparent colors appear luminous and higher keyed in value over a white enamel.

Enameled steel can be used for all types of decorative accessories for the home: serving trays, ash trays, bowls, vases, wall tile, table tops, flooring, lighting fixtures, and inlays for wood cabinets. Its greatest commercial use today is in certain wall panels for building exteriors. This metal offers a fine, sturdy base for sectional wall decorations and huge murals.

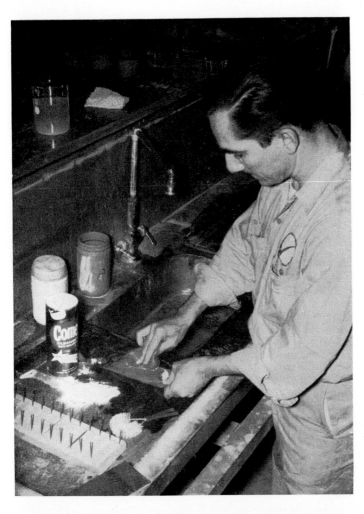

preparing
steel for
enameling

Small sheets of 18 gauge steel are cleaned with scouring powder, steel wool, and water. The metal is then rinsed in water and dried, preparatory to enameling.

The piece of steel can then be enameled easily by dipping or spraying. Here it is being dipped into a basin of dark blue ground coat, slush enamel.

During the dipping operation, the piece is held on the edges by the fingers and shaken a couple of times to get rid of excess enamel. This process covers both sides at the same time. The piece is then placed upon a nail board to dry. When dry, it can be handled quite easily by the fingers, without marring the enamel.

Drying can take place in an oven, over a hot plate, or on top of the furnace. When the piece is completely moisture free, it is ready to be fired for three minutes at 1500°F.

After the ground coat has been fired and the piece has cooled, it is ready for a white coat. The dipping and firing operations are the same. This gleaming white surface acts as a base for the later application of designs, transparent colors or textures.

aluminum

ALTHOUGH TODAY aluminum is one of our most common and inexpensive metals, it was extremely expensive a half century ago because of refining costs.

Aluminum has many advantages. It is one of the lightest metals in common use, weighing about one-third as much as steel. It resists corrosive action from the atmosphere more than any other metal, and in its pure, soft state it is very malleable. Fourteen to sixteen gauge aluminum can be formed and shaped by hand almost as easily as cold-rolled annealed copper. Aluminum is sold in both sheets and rolls of assorted sizes and widths.

Within the past few years, solders and suitable fluxes have been perfected which permit the successful soldering or welding of aluminum.

In purchasing sheet aluminum, the 12 or 14 gauge thickness is probably best; however, thinner gauges can be used successfully. In sheet or roll form, always ask for the purest type, No. 3003 or No. 6061 formerly known as 3S and 61S. If a more solid, three-dimensional project calls for an aluminum casting, one must purchase, or request the foundry to use, No. 43 alloy.

45

enameling aluminum

THROUGH THE EXTENSIVE RESEARCH of several American companies in the past eight or ten years, a low temperature, vitreous enamel for aluminum has been developed. This discovery has satisfied a long felt need for an impervious protective color coating for this metal, permitting the full utilization of aluminum's desirable lightweight properties.

Since aluminum melts at approximately 1200°F., these enamels had to be compounded to fuse at 950 to 1000°F. over a firing period of ten minutes.

Cleaning and pre-heating

Aluminum must be cleaned and pickled properly before enamel will adhere and fire onto it successfully. A bath of hot caustic soda and water for a period of about twenty minutes will give the necessary alkaline etch to the metal. In some instances a combination of chromate salts and the same caustic soda and water solution is used. After the metal has been pickled, it must be washed with clean water and dried. Then a pre-heating in the furnace for ten minutes at a temperature of 1000°F. is necessary. This is the only metal which requires this form of pre-heating, but one cannot enamel aluminum successfully without this operation. Subjecting

46

this metal to heat produces a dull satin surface which allows the enamel better adherence.

Types of enamel

There are two types of enamel made for aluminum, one containing alkaline and high lead, and one without lead. When working with either type, it is advisable to wear a dust respirator over the nose and mouth and to wash the hands and face thoroughly afterward.

Application of the enamel

Unlike enamels ground for use on steel and copper, aluminum enamels must be fine enough to pass through a 325 mesh sieve. This is almost as fine as face powder. These enamels cannot be sifted on dry but are applied to the metal by dipping or spraying. These enamels are purchased in the liquid state ready for use.

If the metal is to be dipped into the enamel with the excess shaken off, the procedure is the same as that used in applying slush enamels to copper or steel.

If regular spray equipment is available, using spray gun or air brush and compressor is the ideal means of application; if not, the new Sprayon Jet-Pak container that operates with propellant refrigerant gas can be used (see illustration). This enamel can be thinned with water if necessary and when it has been well stirred, it can be placed in the glass jar section of the sprayer. One must be careful not to allow the enamel to dry out in the valve hole or spray head of the Jet-Pak. If this does happen, it can be cleaned out by running water through it.

Just enough enamel should be sprayed onto the metal to cover it completely—not too heavy or thick. The moisture can then be dried out of the piece by holding it in front of the open door of the furnace. When firing, always use a pyrometer in order to maintain the temperature at 1000°F. A watch can be used to time the piece ten full minutes while it is in the furnace.

Designs and surface effects

A paper adhesive stencil can be used for cutting suitable designs, as illustrated. The entire piece of metal should be covered with the stencil and the design cut out with razor blade or mat-cutting knife and then peeled off the surface of the piece. The cut-out areas will receive the enamel spray, and the masked sections can be polished later with fine steel wool or a buffer. A contrast of the polished metal and the fired color makes an unusual surface.

The student will find that enameled aluminum offers possibilities for unusual accidental effects. It has been my experience that upon the second or third firing of enameled aluminum, masses of extremely fine hair lines will appear. These can be an asset or a detriment depending upon what one expects as the end result. Once a piece of aluminum is coated with an opaque white, black or colored enamel and fired, the surface is then ready for any type of decoration, including liquid gold, platinum, silver, lusters or other textures. Practically all decorating techniques so effective in steel and copper enameling can be used with success on a surface of aluminum.

To date, there is only one transparent clear enamel for aluminum which, when fired, reveals the surface of the metal underneath. This enamel can be used most successfully when the surface of the metal has a deep etched or engraved design. A great assortment of transparent colors will undoubtedly be developed in due time.

The possibilities for artistic expression with aluminum and aluminum enamels are as great as with copper or steel enamels. Much time, thought, and experimentation are required to get the most from this medium. Precise cutting of stencils and the successful application and firing of the enamel can produce works of fine craftsmanship. For the ambitious professional, architectural panels as well as three-dimensional abstract sculpture of sheet or cast aluminum present a great challenge. A beginner's book on enameling metals would not be complete without a chapter on aluminum.

A piece of clean, pre-heated aluminum is covered with a sheet of "stickback" stencil paper. After sticking it securely to the metal, a design is cut out with the use of a stencil or mat-cutting knife.

working with aluminum

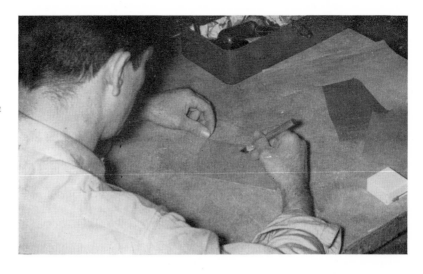

With several triangular areas cut out, the stencil is then ready to be sprayed with aluminum enamel through a Jet-Pak sprayer. The amount of spray should not be too heavy but just enough to completely cover the aluminum. After drying the moisture from the enamel, the piece is ready to be fired. When spraying any enamel, it is a good precaution to wear a respirator over the nose and mouth. A spray booth with an exhaust fan should be used (see accompanying illustration).

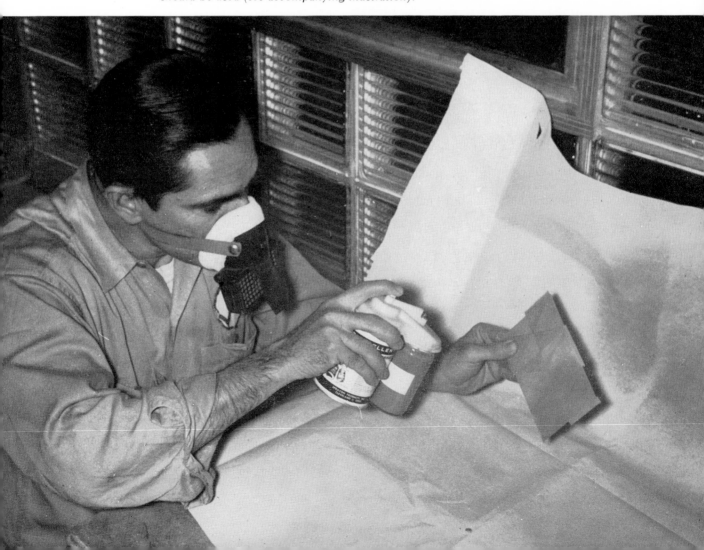

This Craftool spray booth is ideal for school or studio use. It is equipped with an exhaust fan. Model #2019—24 inches wide, 28 inches deep, and 28 inches high. Over-all height, 66 inches.

A temporary spray booth made from a corrugated box, while not ideal, may prove adequate for a simple project.

The light areas on the small plaque are the bare aluminum from which the stencil paper has been removed; the darker spaces are the enamel. The asbestos mittens are used to handle the enamel when it comes from the furnace. Firing temperature should be 1000°F. for a period of ten minutes.

After the piece has cooled, the bare metal areas can be cleaned and polished with fine steel wool, scouring powder, and water. To produce a bright, polished surface, a motor-driven buffer can be used.

This piece of aluminum foil, only .005 of an inch thick, has been sprayed with opaque enamel and fired. This thin sheet can then be cut, bent or twisted without fracturing the enamel. Such a flexible material presents unlimited uses.

*Small enameled alumi-
num, steel or copper plaques
make ideal covers or tops for
leather, metal, and wood
cigarette boxes.*

*Vitreous enamel on
aluminum plaques, bowls, plates
and ash trays. These line designs
were made by painting liquid,
silver, platinum, and gold onto a
fired enamel colored surface.
Other inlaid colors were applied
with a brush.* BY THE AUTHOR,
1957

LEFT: *The body of the bird is bent over the aluminum rod and fastened securely with set screws.*

RIGHT: *Individual sections of the bird being pre-heated in the furnace to burn off grease and other foreign matter on the metal. This operation takes ten minutes with the furnace temperature set at 1,000°F.*

making
aluminum
birds

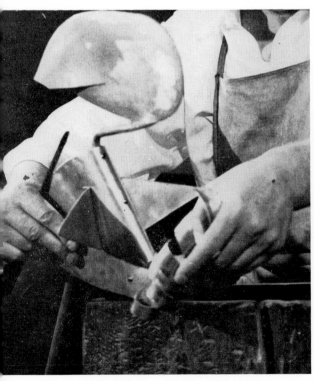

The head and wing of the bird rest against the sink while the tail section is dipped into opaque enamel.

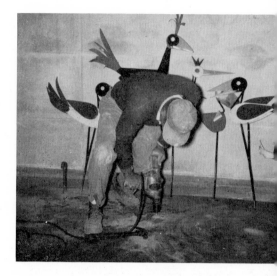

TOP: *Holes were drilled into the floor of the pool. Rods holding the finished birds were inserted and cemented in place.*

CENTER: *A wide enamel aluminum band was fastened to the base of the birds to give them support.*

BOTTOM: *The designer of these aluminum birds arranges them as garden pieces.*

54

Edward and Thelma Frazier Winter pose with their family of colorfully enameled birds.

decorative techniques

ONLY WHEN THE STUDENT THOROUGHLY UNDERSTANDS his materials and their methods of application will he be able to gain the control necessary to realize his creative intentions. Technical perfection is achieved by mastering this sequence of steps necessary for creating an enamel piece: shaping the metal, cleaning it, applying the enamel, drying and firing, polishing the edges or other exposed metal areas.

The art of enameling metals offers numerous decorative techniques. Since this book is directed toward the beginner, only the simplest ones will be illustrated, particularly those that deal with applied decoration on a fired enamel surface. All types of enamel surfaces lend themselves to assorted color, design, and texture treatments. A clean-looking, opaque white surface will probably serve the student best, inasmuch as all transparent colors will appear bright and luminous when fired on top of it. If one is working on a warm, opaque gray surface, the choice of other opaque colors would range in value from light to dark. A glossy jet black surface provides a base for a wide range of opaque colors, including gray and white. All lusters, including liquid gold, silver, and platinum are effective when fired over a black surface.

The accompanying photographs demonstrate the simplest and most effective techniques for the beginning student and the teacher, including stencil, silk screen, drawing pencil, sgraffito, and compass and ruling pen for the application of precious metals.

Students who are interested in the more complex techniques such as cloisonné, champlevé or other traditional forms of enamel art may refer to my book *Enamel Art on Metals* for detailed description.

56

stencil and painting

"Stickback" is a pressure-sensitive paper made for
stenciling. It can be purchased in a large roll, and
the desired amount for individual use cut out.
This paper has crepe backing that can be removed
before the paper is attached to the enamel tiles.

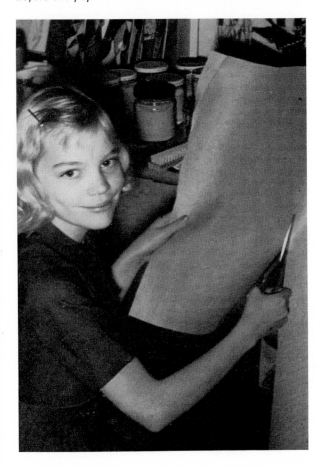

After the design is drawn with a pencil on the
stencil paper, it can be cut out with a single-edge
razor blade attached to a wooden handle or a mat-
cutting knife. Any smooth, hard surface will serve
for precise cutting of the stencil.

A five and one-half inch, 80 mesh brass sieve
is used to apply the 80 mesh enamel to the tiles.
The tiles are wet with a thin gum tragacanth solution that serves to hold the dry powder. Transparent lumps of frit and white enamel strings can be
used to give unusual textural effects.

A simple positive and negative stencil is cut for
another project consisting of five oblong black
enamel tiles. An opaque white or light gray will
be used to contrast with the black surface.

One section of the panel is being placed in the furnace. The pyrometer is in the triangular base of the furnace and is set at 1450°F. A firing time of two and one-half minutes will fuse the enamel to the tile. The tile is shown resting on a chrome triangular metal trivet.

After the "stickback" paper stencil has been pressed onto the smooth surface of the fired tiles, a thin gum tragacanth solution is sprayed on with a mouth blower. The 80 mesh enamel is sifted on. If the surface is still too dry, a gentle spray of clear water can be sprayed on. The stencil can then be removed and each tile dried and fired.

59

This Sprayon Jet-Pak is ideal for spraying thin gum tragacanth solution or any enamel that is extremely finely ground (325 mesh). Silk screening enamel paste thinned with turpentine or any other overglaze colors can be used. Also, aluminum enamels, with proper thinning, work well. This sprayer comes equipped with a four ounce glass container attached to the can of "propellant" compressed gas. This is neither inflammable, nor toxic. Water or proper solvents should be used to keep the needle valve clean.

The Jet-Pak hand sprayer is being used to spray on a thin solution of finely ground black screening paste. Any colored enamel can be used to give interest to other areas of the design, and overlapping of the colors causes no harm.

White string textures, black and yellow green frit, and liquid gold were used to complete the sectional panel. A gentle spray of gum and water will protect the small lumps from falling before drying and firing.

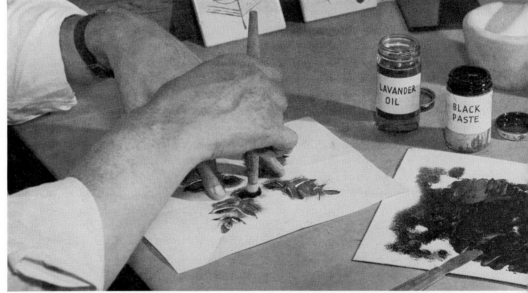

An absorbent paper towel makes a fine stencil for the pouncing of black or other colored screening pastes. A palette knife and naphtha or turpentine can be used for mixing the enamel to the proper consistency. Use a separate brush for each color.

Lifting the paper to show the enamel on the tile. The absorbent paper keeps the enamel from creeping under the edge.

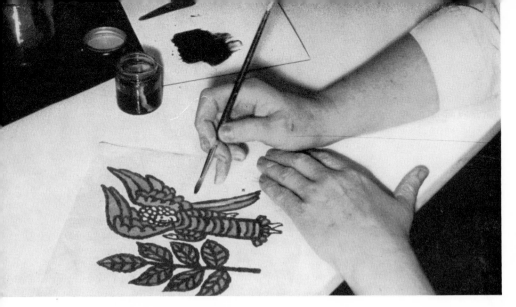

THE THREE WISE MEN *A plaque eighteen inches in diameter, and a panel,* The Juggler, *were made using the stencil technique. Black as well as colored pastes were used in combination with sgraffito.*
THELMA FRAZIER WINTER, 1959

After a bright solid color is applied on the leaves and the angel, a heavy black outline can be painted on with a pointed brush and black paste.

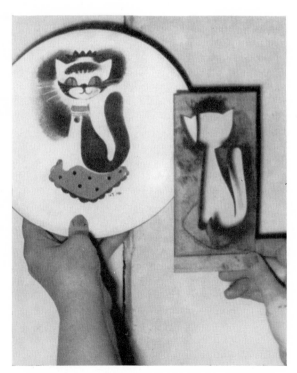

THE KITTEN ON THE CUSHION *Was made with a thin stencil. The dark tone of enamel behind the neck and head of the kitten was achieved by placing the negative part of the stencil on top of the body and pouncing the black enamel around it.*

62

ABOVE: ANGEL FISH *Was made with a "stickback" pressure sensitive stencil, which produces sharp, clean edges. A pocket comb was used to scratch through the enamel for the background. Colors are lemon yellow, gray, green, black, and white.* BY THE AUTHOR, *1934*

BELOW: *Transparent cement was used to apply these plaques to the polished wood surface.*

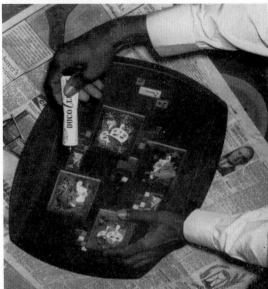

Jewelry, box tops, compacts, and match safes can be made with a variety of techniques: silk screen, stencil, sifting or sgraffito. Lump frit, texture, and precious metals are applied in the usual manner. BY THE AUTHOR, *1952*

63

PORTRAIT OF A GIRL *Painter's technique.*
STEPHANIE KOCHMANN, 1958.

Ash Tray, orange and brown. Painter's technique.   CAROLE SMITH, 1958.
Enamel on copper picture. Painter's technique.   GEORGE KESEGICK, 1958.
Ash Tray, Green, black and yellow. Painter's technique. RUTH DANIELS, 1958.

Portrait Studies. Painter's technique.
OBEDIAH FISHER, 1958.

Silk Screen Print. Orange and Brown.
HOWARD FOX, 1958.

COUNTRY COUSIN *These playful creatures were made by pouncing gray enamel through a stencil. Chartreuse lumps of transparent frit and liquid gold were used for accents. The background is opaque white.* THELMA FRAZIER WINTER, *1956*

Natural forms such as butterflies, flowers, and ferns are simplified for decoration. At first glance the design seems to be flat or on one plane, but it actually has three dimensions, with each leaf or flower carefully modeled in color and light and dark values. BY THE AUTHOR, *1942*

slip or slush trailing

THIS IS ONE of the simplest techniques devised for the beginner as well as the professional and one that allows great spontaneity in rapid dispensing of liquid slush or slip enamel. While enamel can be easily spread and controlled with a syringe, the eager experimenter may soon find this dispenser too slow and might prefer the faster technique of spooning the enamel on or pouring it out from a long nosed plastic container. A spatula is also a handy tool for spreading the enamel. One must remember that the heavier and thicker the enamel is applied to a surface, the longer time will be required to dry it out before firing.

This free technique can be exploited more fully when both transparent and opaque enamels are used. The 80 mesh transparent enamels can be sprinkled on with the fingers and the liquid opaque placed against it to create unusual pattern arrangements.

BELOW LEFT: *Unusual effects to those found in nature can be produced with the syringe applicator. This composition, 20 by 20 inches, is in gray, brown, green, black, and white. White strings and red accents are added.* BY THE AUTHOR, 1940 *Collection Cleveland Museum of Art*

BELOW: ABSTRACTION *Enamel on steel panel, 30 by 35 inches, produced with liquid and string and lump textures. Colors are pink, gray, white, and black.* BY THE AUTHOR, 1941

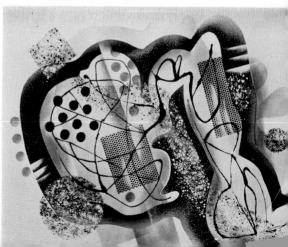

A rubber ball syringe can be filled with liquid slush enamel and used as an applicator for tiles and panels. The unusual, freely expressed surfaces that are possible with this technique afford fun for beginner and professional alike. Enamel should be kept air tight in glass jars or plastic bags when not in use.

Large and medium size lumps of transparent frit will give depth and richness if fired on a copper surface. When small tiles are fired in a flat position the first time and supported almost vertically on the trivet (firing support) the second time, the enamels run together in a variegated pattern.

This is, indeed, a technique for the experimenter or the abstractionist, a person with imagination who likes to produce accidental effects and who has learned to use the heat of the furnace as a means to this end.

sgraffito

AMONG THE PROCESSES and techniques described in this book, sgraffito offers the widest range of creative expression for the beginner and advanced student.

Sgraffito is an Italian word meaning "scratched." In the past, this technique was used primarily in the decoration of pottery rather than enamels.

The decoration was produced by scratching a design through a thin coat of clay, which contrasted with the color of the ware. As early as 1933, I adapted this technique to the decoration of enamel bowls and plaques by first firing a coat of white enamel to the surface of the bowl and then applying a thin coat of black enamel over it. When this coat dried or was still in a damp condition, a design could be scratched through it to expose the white layer underneath. This, in effect, produced a white linear design on a dark background. The technique is so adaptable that it can be used in many ways, including white line drawings, decorative designs using natural forms, such as birds, animals, fruit, leaves, and flowers, to mention only a few; or it may be used to create abstract dark and light patterns. To carry the decorative possibilities even further, colored enamels or liquid golds and lusters can be added for additional variety and change of surface texture and color.

A surface suitable for sgraffito design can be prepared in the following manner: fire a coating of opaque white enamel to the metal, then spray or dip slush enamel of black or another color over it. This application should not be too heavy—a brisk shaking with wrist action will serve to thin the enamel on the surface. When it has dried or is still in a slightly damp condition, scratch through the surface with a sharp, pointed stick or sharp dental tool. Using this scratch technique, extremely fine or heavy lines

69

These plastic window templates are valuable aids in producing linear designs and precise patterns. They can be purchased at any art supply store.

can be produced, depending upon the kind of pointed tool you use. These white lines appearing through a darker enamel will be as effective as the reverse of this procedure; that is, if a base coat of black is used and a white enamel is applied over the top, the result will be black lines upon a white surface.

The coarse 80 mesh grind enamel is not too suitable for this technique; one must use the slush enamel that has been ground to 250 to 350 mesh. The small amount of clay in which this enamel is ground will allow the piece to be handled gently after it has dried without the enamel coming off.

Experiments can also be made by applying the same opaque enamel to the base copper, then scratching the design through to reveal the surface of the metal, and applying and firing a transparent enamel over the top.

The sharpened opposite end of a brush serves as a tool for creating sgraffito lines with the plastic templates. A slush enamel dipped or sprayed onto a white fired plaque is drawn into. Excess enamel powder can be blown away.

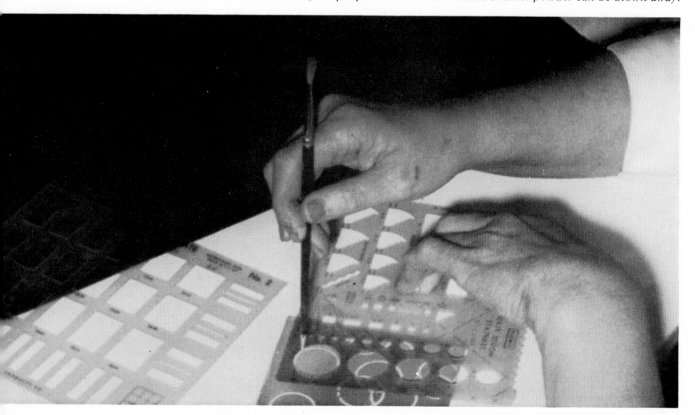

FORMS IN SPACE *An enamel steel panel, 28 by 10 inches, using the template and sgraffito techniques. Liquid gold and sheets of silver foil were applied in some areas of the design. The colors are blue, green, yellow, brown, black, and white.* BY THE AUTHOR, *1955*

These early works of the author were executed in sgraffito. The top of the brass box is enameled copper. 1934

The sgrafitto technique, when handled freely, is one of the finest available to the enameler. In these small decorated pieces the enamel colors were applied over a fired white surface. The line drawings were made with a sharply pointed wooden tool. THELMA FRAZIER WINTER, *1958*

71

RIGHT: *A white sgraffito design can be effective as a
border on a copper-footed
bowl. The edge is opaque
brown, and the interior is
transparent brown.* BY THE
AUTHOR, *1941*

BELOW: *This three-part panel,
18 by 27 inches, shows a
spontaneous white and black
line design. Accents are red
and yellow-green.* BY THE
AUTHOR, *1948*

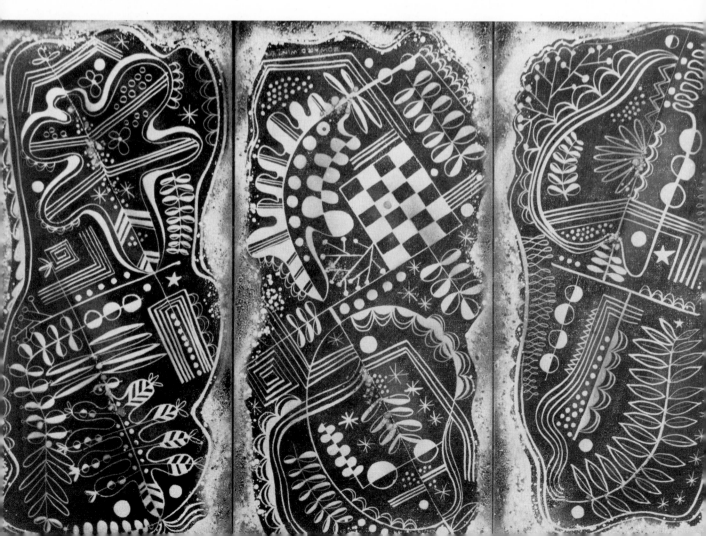

drawing with a white line

A NEW WHITE PENCIL made of a specially compounded material allows great freedom of expression for the enamelist. This tool is one of my own developments, which has proved very popular.

These pencils are effective only when used on a dark toned or black fired enamel surface. To be able to draw in this spontaneous manner will delight the beginner or the professional draughtsman accustomed to working in line.

This technique is most suited to large surfaces; the worker will soon discover that there is no advantage to using it in small areas. Once the white drawing is applied to the small panel or sectional tiles, it can be fired at a temperature of approximately 1450°F. for two and a half minutes without disappearing. Enamel colors or metallic lusters can then be applied with a brush to fill in areas of the composition. (Refer to chapters on these techniques.)

Student shown laying out a white line drawing on a series of black enameled steel tiles. The white ceramic pencil can also be used to number the back of each tile so that, after firing, they can be laid down in their proper place.

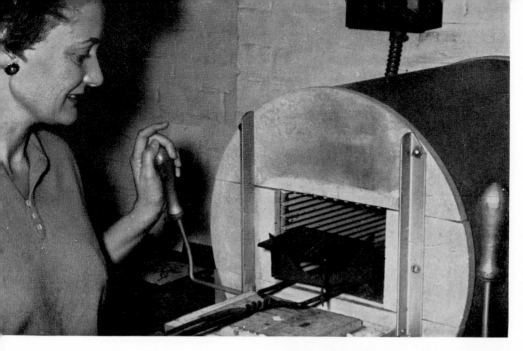

Tiles are fired one at a time with the furnace set at 1450°F. The white lines do not fade during this two minute firing.

After the tiles have been fired and cooled, they can be decorated with painted enamel colors or liquid precious metals.

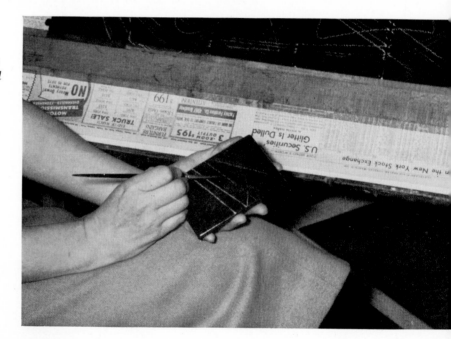

An interesting pattern is created when liquid gold and an assortment of enamel colors are filled in between the white lines. A subtle gradation of tone is produced by the black base enamel appearing through some of the colored surfaces.

silk screen printing

SILK SCREEN PRINTING with both tempera and oil paints has enjoyed many years of popularity in high schools. In fact, this applied art technique is so popular that several small silk screen printing kits are now available in art supply stores.

Vitreous enamels have now been developed by several manufacturers for silk screening. These enamels are of an extremely fine grind, but instead of using water and clay, as in preparing the slush or slip enamels, they are ground in a pine oil and soybean solution. These silk screen pastes can be ordered from the manufacturer in any quantity desired. A small quantity of this enamel will go a long way, so it is quite inexpensive to use. A half pint will equal one pound, and one quart will be equivalent to four pounds. The price for small quantities will run from two dollars and seventy-five cents to three dollars and twenty-five cents per pound; larger quantities can be purchased for as little as one dollar and fifty cents per pound.

These enamels can be purchased in black and white, and dozens of deep, rich opaque colors, and light pastel shades. Because they are finely ground, they lend themselves to intermixing by the use of a glass slab and a palette knife. White added to a color will lighten its value, and the addition of black will darken it. Some colors, made with transparent base frit, are semi-transparent.

75

Materials

Any art supply store will sell the wood frames, rubber squeegee, and various grades of silk, organdy, dacron or nylon required for silk screen printing. The fine grade silks are quite expensive, but nylon and other cheaper materials will work just as well. No grade of cloth will hold up too long with the vitreous paste being forced through it, as the fine glass particles have a tendency to cut the material. For commercial production and long production runs of enamel printing, a fine stainless steel wire or phosphor bronze cloth is often used.

Process

A small, flat enameled tile or panel is used as a surface to receive the screen printing. The size of the tile or panel will depend upon the size of your furnace opening; however, several inch-square tiles can be placed close together upon the table so that one large screen can be used to print the design on all the tiles in one operation. The tiles can then be picked up one at a time and fired. In printing several colors, one must use a separate screen for each color, but if there is a slight overlapping of one color with another in printing, it will usually fire out well. Turpentine is used as a thinner and for cleaning tools and screens. The hard rubber squeegee is used to pull the enamel across the screen.

Since cutting the film stencil and adhering it to the silk is done as in ordinary silk screen printing, we will not describe the process here.

Firing the enamel

Most silk screen pastes and colors are formulated to fuse at temperatures of from 1300 to 1350°F. The enamel surface upon which they are to be fired, however, has received the customary 1450 to 1500° firing. These enamel pastes fuse within two to two-and-a-half minutes. A piece to be fired should be held at the open door of the furnace until all the volatile oils have been smoked away, and then placed in the heat and fired. If opaque enamel steel tiles are used as a base for the screened designs, at least a two or two-and-a-half minute firing time will be required. Enameled copper tiles will not require so long a firing.

A teacher instructing his students in the silk screen technique. The screen is placed tightly against the white enamel panel, and the black enamel paste is squeezed through the silk with a rubber squeegee.

Unusual effects

Anyone experienced with serigraph or silk screen printing knows the possibilities for unusual effects and textures. The silk can be spattered or stippled with glue or other adhesive material that will not be affected by the solvent. Wire threads can also be glued to the silk to produce unusual hair-line textures in each print. Other interesting surface effects can be obtained by screening clear varnish onto the fired enamel surface and dry-sifting an enamel powder onto it. This tacky surface will hold the powder secure and burn away in the intense heat. This same varnish surface can be used to hold reflective glass beads or balls, enamel strings or bits of foil prior to firing.

Both teacher and students will be happy to learn that most of the silk screens and frames previously used in the classroom can be used equally well with enamel screening paste. Small sections of a large screen design can be masked out with tape and reproduced in enamel on a tile or any other flat piece of enameled metal.

Screen Process Methods of Reproduction by Bert Zahn is one of the most informative books on this subject. It is published by Frederick J. Drake and Company, Chicago, Illinois.

The lifted screen reveals three sets of dancing figures. After the panel has been fired (at about 1400°F.) to protect the design, further drawing or color can be added.

A *shallow container can be used to hold the black enamel paste; and a palette knife, to keep it well mixed and "tacky." The paste should not be applied too thin. The lifted screen reveals a leaf design.*

A *pointed camel's hair brush is used to touch up portions of the leaf.*

A colorful enamel Christmas card can be made, using several screens through which several colors are applied.

The author's Christmas card of 1933 (enamel on copper) and three other possibilities for enamel Christmas greetings.

A successful silk screen design in orange, white, and brown, suitable for reproduction in enamel. HOWARD FOX, 1958

A bold rhythmic pattern using the silk screen printing process. ROBERT NOVAK, 1958

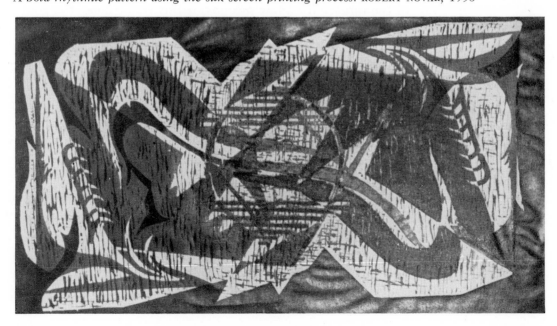

liquid gold, silver, platinum, and lusters

AN ASSORTMENT OF PRECIOUS METALS, including gold, silver, platinum, and lusters, is available on the market in liquid form for the enameler. These metals have been reduced to liquid form by being dissolved and held in suspension by volatile oils. They may be purchased ready for use from manufacturing sources listed in the appendix of this book.

These liquid metals and lusters may be applied with a camel's hair brush. As a first step in fusing them to the surface of the enamel, the worker must remember to "smokeaway" or burn off solvents and suspending oils by holding the piece at the entrance of the furnace for a few seconds. If this is not done, the gold will quickly burn up along with the burning of the oils. When the smoking period has ended, the piece is ready to be placed into the furnace. The most suitable temperature for this type of firing is from 1350 to 1375°F., at a firing time not exceeding two to two-and-a-half minutes. If, under these conditions, the resultant metal surface is dull or not bright enough, try the same firing time with the furnace set at 1400 to 1450°F. I would, however, suggest that test samples first be made in your furnace.

Great care must be used in the application of these liquid metals. First of all, the surface must be thoroughly cleaned of dust, impurities, and especially perspiration or oily marks from the fingers; otherwise, the liquid gold will crackle or tear, preventing a smooth, solid surface; or it may disappear altogether from these uncleaned areas. Other defects will appear if small amounts of gold

82

The Sprayon Jet-Pak is fun to work with. Liquid gold is sprayed onto a fired white enamel plaque. To produce white crossing lines, strings were stretched across the surface of the plaque. Before being fired (for two minutes at 1400°F) the piece must be placed at the opening of the furnace door to "smoke away" the oils.

Liquid gold is being applied with the compass. All metallic lusters, as well as thinned screening enamels, can be applied in the same manner. Ruling pens are used for straight lines. Pieces of masking tape serve to anchor the point of the compass.

are accidentally transferred from the fingers or brushes to the surface of the enamel, as they will leave small purplish smudges when fired.

A good cleaning agent for the surface of the enamel as well as for brushes, pens, and other application equipment is methanol or wood alcohol. Other cleaning agents are carbontetrachloride and nitrobenzene.

It is a good policy to clean brushes immediately after use; and one must remember to use a separate brush for each metal, since any intermixture of gold, silver or platinum will produce a dirty, defective surface.

Precious metals sell for approximately twenty dollars to twenty-five dollars for one hundred grams, but they can be purchased in smaller quantities from any ceramic supply company. In some respects they are quite economical, since they go a long way in covering surfaces, and their use is rewarding because it gives a fine quality finish to any work of art.

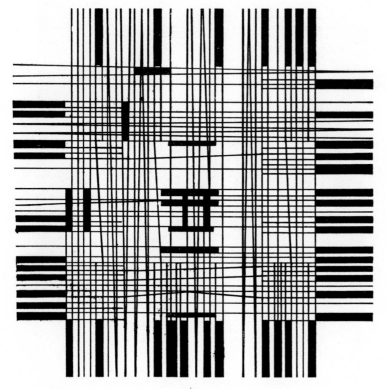

An interesting pattern of straight lines of varying thicknesses made with the ruling pen.

Liquid gold can be applied with a small, pointed camel's hair brush over a fired opaque or transparent enamel surface. These pieces, by the author, are in gold and transparent brown.

textures

TEXTURE MEANS CHARACTER OF SURFACE: smooth, rough, coarse, fine, hard or soft. Subtleties, variations, and contrasts in surface treatment enrich the object and contribute much to the visual and tactile qualities of the artist's work.

Textures can be used to dramatize subject matter, whether realistic or abstract; but the abstractionist can probably profit most by them.

The tremendous possibilities inherent in the tasteful application of textures, previously unused by traditional enamelists, have perhaps played the most important part in attracting the interest of students and professionals to the art of enameling.

My earliest bowls, plaques, and panels contained textures, since I had learned many years ago to make small pot smeltings of enamels and from this molten batch of glass to produce my own thread, strings, balls and assorted size lumps. These interestingly shaped pieces of enamel can be picked up with the fingers and placed anywhere on an enamel surface one wants to fuse them.

Enamel suppliers now furnish an assortment of these enamel pieces.

86

ABOVE: *An ash tray is dipped into a basin of opaque gray slush enamel. Two or three sharp shakes of the wrist will remove the excess enamel.*

RIGHT: *Small, colorful black, green, and yellow enamel threads can be applied to the wet enamel surface, which can then be dried and fired. These fine threads, pioneered by the author, are now available on the market.*

The student with imagination will discover other items such as copper and silver wire, silver and gold foil, wheels and small springs from watches, and many other metal findings which he can melt onto the surface of an enamel piece to produce unusual effects.

Medium size lumps of opaque white enamel frit are suitable for creating textures. They can be purchased from the enamel supplier.

Objects of the type mentioned fuse more securely onto a surface of transparent enamel on heavy gauge copper, and if the metal is of 12 to 14 gauge in thickness, small sheets of glass can be fused onto it successfully.

Copper is also the best metal upon which to produce crackled or tearing surfaces in the enamel. Dipping or spraying a slush or slip opaque enamel over a fired transparent surface will result in this effect upon firing. Whether the result is a thin or wide tear or a separation will depend upon the length of time the piece is left in the heat. A two minute firing time at 1500°F. will produce a fine crackle, and four minutes will make a wide one.

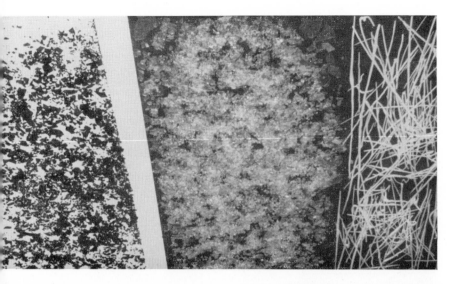

Large strings of white enamel and white and black flake enamels can be applied with the fingers. Gum tragacanth can be used to keep them stationary until the piece is fired.

Large and medium size lumps of frit and small glass balls or beads can give interesting tactile surfaces to an enamel. A pocket comb produces rhythmic patterns.

CALLA LILIES *An enamel on steel panel, 30 by 30 inches, showing the white strings and the small glass balls fused onto the surface.* BY THE AUTHOR, *1941,* Collection, Everson Museum of Art, Syracuse, N. Y.

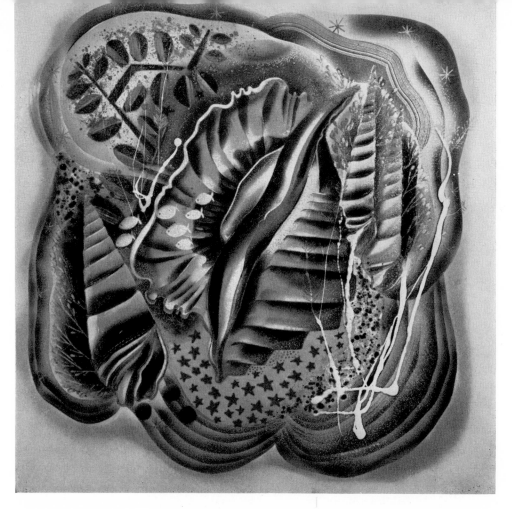

PINK SHELLS *This composition, 36 inches square, shows the effective use of applied string textures, lumps of colored frit, and a speckled effect produced from the overlapping and fusion of transparent and opaque enamels. The colors are pink, brown, green, yellow, black, and gold.* BY THE AUTHOR, 1952

design

WHILE IT IS NOT THE PURPOSE of a beginner's book on enameling to deal extensively with design principles, it is important for the beginner to know something about certain basic shapes.

The circle, the square, and the triangle are among the simplest shapes one can use to create interesting and effective conventional designs. There has always been a great need for simplicity of applied design in enamels; so by suggesting the occasional use of these shapes, we may serve to make the work of the beginner look more professional. These three shapes can be most effectively used by applying the elementary principles of repetition, alternation, parallelism, opposition, and balance (as shown in the accompanying reproductions). One can readily see how effectively these design elements could be used on bracelets, cuff links, earrings, box tops, bowls, and ash trays.

A student with imagination can catch the eye of the viewer with such decorative and stylized effects as playing horizontal lines against vertical ones, playing mass against mass, using complementary color schemes or a subtle sequence of grays, white, and black. Greater and lesser space intervals between design elements add to the general interest.

These fundamental principles of design can be taught quite easily to any student, encouraging him to develop an intuitive and spontaneous sense of design that expresses his own experience and personality.

While we have been thinking of these three elements in relation to applied decoration, we might add that they offer fine possibilities for the basic shapes of utilitarian objects.

OPPOSITE *This footed bowl illustrates the unique effect produced when a transparent brown enamel has first been applied and fused to a copper bowl and an opaque white slush or slip enamel is applied and fired over it. As the brown melts and begins to flow slightly, it pulls the white enamel, causing this crackle effect. No two pieces will ever crackle in exactly the same manner.*

The circle, the square, and the triangle can be sub-divided to create simple areas or used in combination to produce more complex patterns.

92

The square, the circle, and the triangle are used as the basic shape to create these all-over patterns, which would lend themselves to tile or panel designs.

93

The basic circle form is modified by the use of straight, curved, and S-curve line combinations and also combined with triangles.

The triangle is combined with straight, curved, S-curve, and spiral lines and with circles of different sizes to form other shapes. Alternating sequences of light and dark are also used.

Repetition and alternation are used to form border patterns.

the artist
and his
public

A STUDENT WHO SHOWS a decided aptitude for enameled metals, even under the handicap of a small classroom furnace and simple equipment, should realize that a wonderful prospect for a gainful future is possible.

We live in a period when both architects and interior designers are re-appraising the value of art for their professions. Artists and craftsmen are finding a great demand for their work and the added satisfaction of having it placed where people can see and appreciate it.

Every professional example of art reproduced in this book shows the artist's control over his product from the initial impetus of the idea to its completion. A relationship and responsibility to the object created and to the person who will enjoy it is essential to the craftsman.

This has been my philosophy for more than thirty years. I discovered early that the American public does not necessarily beat a path to the door of a fine craftsman; that if the craftsman wants his product introduced to the public, he must make them aware of it.

While a complete volume could be written on this subject, it is enough to say that any production, selling or distribution of enamels must be conducted in a small way at first by creating one outlet and maintaining it satisfactorily before another is attempted. One must always remember that an artist must perfect his craft through years of study and work before he is ready for a market.

It is never too early for the young student to become dedicated to his craft and learn the use of tools and materials. I know of no material available to the young artist which is better suited to our times and to our needs in decoration than enameled metals. The accompanying examples of tables, store displays, and murals give an idea of the potential of this medium.

Enamels have many practical uses, such as these colorful enamel-on-steel tops for wooden and wrought iron tables. A chromium steel bands trims the table at right.

Transparent enamel-on-copper plaques make colorful and practical table tops. A hole is cut in this wooden table to support the plaque on its wide rim.

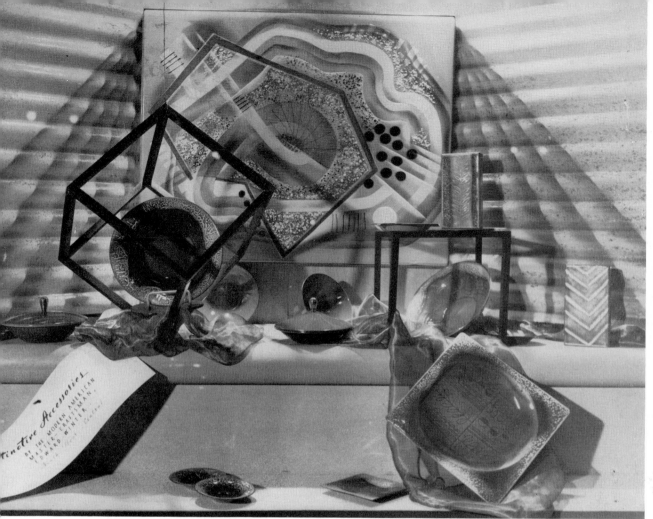

JOHN WANAMAKER, Philadelphia

The craftsman's work reaches the public through store displays. BY THE AUTHOR

HALLE BROS. CO., Cleveland, Ohio

This colorful enamel steel mural, designed and executed by the author, tells the story of the Cleveland suburbs' water purification program. It was designed as a simple, schematic plan so that visiting school children and general public could readily understand the scientific process. The mural, which is composed of forty-two 16 gauge steel panels, is five feet high and twenty-four feet long. The panels were fired for three minutes each, at a temperature of from 1450 to 1500°F., in the laboratories of the Ferro Corporation in Cleveland. The author holds the full color sketch.

some points on working
with enamels

1. Classroom projects should consist of working with one metal during a semester. Trying to enamel several metals at one time may result in utter confusion.

2. The beginner will achieve the best results when applying and firing opaque enamels. To obtain good results with transparent enamels requires more time and experience.

3. Opaque enamels can be applied to all specified metals. Transparent enamels show off the polished metal surface of copper, silver, and aluminum. Steel must be silver plated to show clearly through a transparent enamel.

4. Heavy gum tragacanth applications will cloud up and kill a transparent enamel. Use in extremely thin state for best results. Flake agar or glycerine (available in all drug stores) can also be used.

5. Opaque white enamel if applied too thin to copper will turn slightly green in the firing. To produce an even surface, two separate sifting applications may be necessary, each one fired at about 1400°F.

6. Any one of the several hundreds of transparent enamels available on the market can be applied (by 80 mesh sifting) over opaque white. Colors thus applied will appear lighter in tone than when applied directly on copper.

100

7. Transparent enamel colors which can be fired directly onto copper are dark blue, browns, and green. Ruby, purple, pink, yellow, gray, and light blue must be applied and fused over a flux (clear colorless enamel). The flux protects the delicate shades of some colors and prevents the chemical components of others from being affected by the copper under firing.

8. An opaque orange fired directly onto copper will produce a greenish cast. To obtain a clean, true color, opaque orange should be fired over opaque white.

9. If the enamel pops off on the first firing, it is due to dampness. Slush enamels require fifteen to twenty minutes to dry before being fired; and dry sifting enamel, when dampened properly, requires at least a half hour's drying over a hot plate or in an oven.

10. Before firing an enamel for the second time, it should be heated thoroughly. If cracking appears in the enamel when entering the heat, the fine cracks will usually heal satisfactorily. If not, you have faulty copper or the metal is too thin. At least 18 gauge copper should be used.

11. Don't settle for the happy accident, saying, "I wanted it to tear and crackle," when you were wishing for a perfect surface. It will take time and experience, but make the enamel do your bidding.

12. Don't get impatient and rush your enamel into the furnace; haste really makes waste in this art. Give all work loving thought and care.

13. A small enameling department should have separate areas for four distinct functions: forming the metals, cleaning the metals, applying the enamel, and firing. The enameling and firing section should be kept absolutely clear of dust, dirt, bits of steel wool, etc.

14. Knowing your furnace temperature is extremely important. Setting a temperature too high or forgetting a piece in the furnace may result in a "one of a kind" effect by the running and dripping of the enamel. Technical perfection and exacting surfaces are easier to produce when furnace heat is not too high.

15. In furnaces you get what you pay for. The best functioning furnaces for classroom or studio use will cost approximately two hundred and fifty dollars to three hundred dollars. Furnaces in this size and price range will assure you many years of satisfactory service.

16. It takes only two or three minutes to fire an enamel, so stay with your furnace at all times. A watch or interval timer (similar

CARL A. RUDISILL LIBRARY
LENOIR RHYNE COLLEGE

to an alarm clock) can be used for proper timing. Experienced enamelers learn to gauge their firing time so that they have no need for a timer.

17. Remember that the more concave the piece is, the more the enamel will have a tendency to run down the sides of the metal. The application of enamel should be slightly heavier toward the top of the piece than at the bottom. A furnace that is too hot will also force the enamel to the bottom. Vases and deep bowls are the most difficult shapes to enamel successfully.

18. Enamel bowls can be fired right side up or upside down. The proper trivet or support should be used in each case. Alternating the position of the piece in firing often produces good results.

19. Learning dexterity and control in handling a hot enamel with asbestos gloves is an exciting part of the craft. Red-hot pieces taken from the furnace should be held by the edge in order not to mar the enamel and placed quickly onto a hard asbestos table top.

20. Round bowls can be transformed into oval or square sided pieces by quickly squeezing the piece with asbestos gloved hands within a few seconds after the piece leaves the furnace. Cotton fingered gloves are used to handle enamels when they are in a warm state.

some points on working
with metals

1. All metals must receive enamels that are specifically designed for them. Copper enamels cannot be used on aluminum, nor can aluminum enamel be used on steel or copper.

2. Copper can be formed by hand with suitable irons and hammers. Steel is too hard for hand forming and must be spun or die stamped into desired shapes.

3. Impure copper (used for roofing purposes) cannot be used for enameling. Electrolytic copper (18 gauge) should be used.

4. Aluminum must be pre-heated for ten minutes at 1,000°F. before it is enameled. This removes all surface impurities and leaves a slight film of oxide on the metal, effecting a better bond for the enamel.

5. Lead, tin, and German silver or brass cannot be enameled. These metals are either too soft to withstand the heat or are too impure. Guilder's metal, ninety-five per cent copper and five per cent zinc, can be enameled successfully. Most deep, transparent colors fire well on it without the use of flux. Because of zinc content, this metal cannot be fired more than twice without cracking. Ruby red applied directly will fire out a beautiful cherry color.

6. All metals must be cleaned of dirt and grease (including finger marks) if they are to be enameled successfully. Water, scouring

103

powder, and steel wool with plenty of rubbing action will clean them for successful enameling without the need for acid pickling.

7. Nitric acid and water are used to etch designs into metal (always pour the acid into the water). Asphaltum is used for protecting the part of the design that is not to be etched. This champlevé technique is discussed in my book *Enamel Art on Metals*.

8. Steel that has been cleaned and is not ready for immediate enameling should be wrapped in a clean paper or towel and kept in a dry place so that rust does not form on the piece.

9. Aluminum-plated steel can be enameled with aluminum enamels. It will maintain a flat rigid shape after firing. Sheet aluminum has a tendency to warp slightly on both the first and second firings.

10. To repair an enameled copper bowl, clean out the damaged spot with a carborundum or rubbing stone, rinse with clean water, and apply the same enamel, using gum tragacanth as an adhesive. Dry and fire.

11. Large pieces or sheets of thin metal (under 18 gauge) are difficult to enamel. They will warp in the heat of the furnace, and it is difficult to re-shape them before they cool.

12. Hard silver solder must be used for joining two pieces of copper that are to be enameled, such as a ring foot on a bowl. This soldering can be done in the enameling furnace in 3 minutes at 1500°F.

materials and supplies and where to buy them

Adhesives for Bonding
    Duco Cement, at any hardware store
    E-Pox-Y Cement, at any hardware store
    Miracle Adhesive Corp., 214 East 53rd St., New York 22, N. Y.
    White Tile Cement, at any hardware store

Adhesives for Enameling
    Flake Agar, at most drug stores
    Glycerine, at drug stores
    Gum Tragacanth, at most drug stores

Enamels
FOR COPPER, GOLD, AND SILVER:
    Millenent Co., Geneva, Switzerland
    Schauer & Co., Atzgersdorf St., Vienna, Austria
    Thomas C. Thompson Co., 1539 Deerfield Rd., Highland
        Park, Ill.
    Wengers, Ltd., Etruria, Stoke-on-Trent, England
FOR STEEL, CAST IRON, ALUMINUM, AND FOR SILK SCREENING:
    B. F. Drakenfeld & Co., 45 Park Place, New York 7, N. Y.
    Ceramic Color & Mfg. Co., New Brighton, Penna.
    Chicago Vitreous Enamel Co., Cicero, Ill.

E. I. DuPont de Nemours & Co., Wilmington, Delaware
Ferro Corp., 4150 East 56th St., Cleveland, Ohio
O. Hommel Co., Pittsburgh 30, Penna.
Pemco Corp., Baltimore, Maryland
Thomas C. Thompson Co., 1539 Deerfield Rd., Highland Park, Ill.

Furnaces and Kilns

Electric Hotpak Co., Coltman Avenue at Melrose St., Philadelphia, Penna.
Ferro Corp., 4150 East 56th St., Cleveland, Ohio
Hevi-Duty Electric Co., 4212 Highland Ave., Milwaukee, Wisconsin
Hoskins Mfg. Co., 4435 Lawton Ave., Detroit 8, Michigan
James W. Weldon Co., 2315 Harrison Ave., Kansas City 8, Mo.
L & L Mfg. Co., 804 Mulberry St., Upland, Chester, Penna.
Pereny Equipment Co., Dept. C., 893 Chambers Rd., Columbus, Ohio
Thomas C. Thompson Co., 1539 Deerfield Rd., Highland Park, Ill.

Gloves (cloth finger type & asbestos mittens)

Cloth, at most hardware stores
Asbestos, Ferro Corp., 4150 East 56th St., Cleveland, Ohio
Asbestos, the Des Moines Mfg. Co., Des Moines, Iowa

Jewelry Findings

American Metalcraft Inc., 4100 Belmont Ave., Chicago 41, Ill.
C. R. Hill Co., 35 West Grand River, Detroit 26, Michigan
Immerman and Sons, 1924 Euclid Ave., Cleveland 15, Ohio
Metal Findings Corp., 150 W. 22nd St., New York 11, N. Y.
Sax-Crafts, 1103 N. 3rd St., Milwaukee 3, Wisconsin
T. B. Hagstoz & Co., 707 Sanson St., Philadelphia 6, Penna.
Thomas C. Thompson Co., 1539 Deerfield Rd., Highland Park, Ill.

Lusters, Gold, and Platinum

B. F. Drakenfeld & Co., 45 Park Place, New York 7, N. Y.
Hanovia Chemical Co., Englehard Industries Division, 1 West Central Ave., East Newark, N. J.
Harshaw Chemical Co., 1945 E. 79th St., Cleveland 6, Ohio

Metals
ALUMINUM

Aluminum Co. of America, ALCOA Building, Pittsburgh, Penna.

Reynolds Metals Co., S. 3rd St., Louisville, Kentucky

Refer to local phone directory for distributors

COPPER

Chase Brass and Copper Co. (offices in most cities)

The American Brass Co., Waterbury, Conn.

STEEL AND IRON

American Rolling Mill, Middletown, Ohio (offices in most cities)

Bethlehem Steel Co., Bethlehem, Penna. (offices in most cities)

Inland Steel Co., 38 S. Dearborn St., Chicago, Ill. (subsidiaries in most cities)

U. S. Steel Co., U. S. Steel Building, 525 William Penn Place, Pittsburgh, Penna.

Silk Screen Equipment and Materials

Any art supply store

Silver Foil

(As described fully in *Enamel Art on Metals,* by Edward Winter)

Wehrung & Billmeier Co., 3624 Lincoln Ave., Chicago, Ill.

Spray Equipment, Air Compressors, and Spray Booths

Devilbis Spray Equipment, Ohio Art Metals Co., 2174 E. 9th St., Cleveland, Ohio

Paasche VL Airbrushes, Thomas C. Thompson Co., 1539 Deerfield Rd., Highland Park, Ill.

Craftools, Inc., 396 Broadway, New York 13, N. Y.

Sprayon Products Co., 2075 E. 65th St., Cleveland 3, Ohio

Thayer & Chandler Airbrush Co. (Inquire through local art supply company)

Stencil Paper

Multicraft, Inc., 8617 Carnegie Ave., Cleveland, Ohio

C. O. Dicks Co., 124 Lafayette Place, Plainfield, N. J.

Stilts and Trivets (supports to hold enamels for firing)

Artex Mfg. Co., 4038 Huron Ave., Culver City, Calif.

Atlas Steel Point Stilt Co., 4207 Longshore St., Philadelphia 35, Penna.

Charles H. Draving Co., P. O. Box 26, Feasterville, Penna.

The Potters Supply Co., East Liverpool, Ohio

Thomas C. Thompson Co., 1539 Deerfield Rd., Highland Park, Ill.

Texture Materials

Thomas C. Thompson Co., 1539 Deerfield Rd., Highland Park, Ill.

Edward Winter Studio, 11020 Magnolia Drive, Cleveland 6, Ohio

Tools and Equipment

Allcraft Tool & Supply Co., 11 E. 48th St., New York 17, N. Y.

Ancor Tool & Supply Co., 12 John St., New York 7, N. Y.

Brodhead & Garrett, 4560 E. 71st St., Cleveland, Ohio

C. R. Hill Co., 35 W. Grand River, Detroit 26, Michigan

George H. Fuller & Sons Co., 29 E. Madison Ave., Chicago, Ill.

Immerman and Sons, 1924 Euclid Ave., Cleveland 15, Ohio

Ohio Jewelers Supply Co., 1000 Schofield Bldg., Cleveland 15, Ohio

Paul H. Gesswein & Co., 35 Maiden Lane, New York 38, N. Y.

William Dixon, Inc., 32-42 E. Kinney St., Newark, N. J.

Torches

The Otto Bernz Co., 280 Lyell Ave., Rochester 6, N. Y.

(Bernz-o-matic torch at any hardware or department store)

GENERAL INFORMATION (and source for white drawing pencil)
Edward Winter Studio,

11020 Magnolia Drive, Cleveland 6, Ohio

glossary

ACID

Chemical compound used to clean, etch, or pickle metals; sulphuric or nitric acid with water is used for steel or copper.

AQUA REGIA

A mixture of hydrochloric acid and nitric acid which dissolves gold or platinum.

ARSENIC

An element of the phosphorus group used to give high gloss in transparent enamels.

BALL MILL

A rotating cylindrical grinding mill in which enamel frit is wet-ground, producing liquid "slush" or "slip" enamel.

BUFFING WHEEL

A high speed electric shaft upon which cloth, felt or carborundum rubber wheels can be attached to polish metals.

BUNSEN BURNER

A small gas burner used to fuse enamels to metals when no furnace is available.

CARBORUNDUM

Synthetic carbon produced in hard block form to be held in the hand while stoning the edges of enamels before buffing.

COUNTER ENAMEL

The enamel that is applied and fused to the reverse side of any metal. Keeps metal from warping and aids coefficient of expansion.

COMPASS

A device used to draw circles on paper or other surfaces or in applying precious metals to an enamel surface.

CHROMATE SALTS

Chemical for cleaning aluminum prior to enameling.

DETERGENT

Water soluble cleaning agent. Hot detergents serve to clean grease and dirt from metal surfaces.

DRAWING PENCIL

A specially compounded pencil for drawing white lines on dark or black fired enamel surfaces. Will not burn away in furnace heat.

DRY PROCESS

The technique of sifting enamel powder onto metal by the use of a sieve.

DUSTING

Applying dry enamel in extremely finely ground state to an enamel surface with extremely fine sieve.

EMERY CLOTH

Cloth impregnated with fine or coarse grind emery for smoothing metal surfaces or edges of enamel objects.

ENAMELING IRON

A steel, extremely low in carbon, made especially for enameling. Sold in sheets, rolls, or tubes.

ETCHING

Using sulphuric or nitric acids with water to produce designs in metals; or, the use of alkalies or harsh chemicals for cleaning aluminum or steel prior to enameling.

FINDINGS

All forms of manufactured metal parts or objects that can be used in making jewelry or other art objects.

FIRING

A term used for fusing enamels in a furnace.

FRIT

Small particles of enamel produced when molten enamel pours from a smelter into a tank of water or onto steel slabs.

110

FURNACE

A gas or electric chamber or muffle used for firing enamel onto metal. A "kiln" is used for the firing of claywares.

GAUGE

An index number used to denote the thickness of sheet metal.

GLASS BEADS AND BALLS

Small particles of glass used to produce texture when fired into an enamel surface.

GLASS STRINGS

Threads or strings of drawn-out glass enamel made by pulling molten enamel with an iron rod, and allowing it to cool. Used for textural effects.

GUM TRAGACANTH

A vegetable (seaweed) gum in hard flake form available at most drug stores. A few flakes boiled in water produce a thin adhesive for wetting the copper for dry process application of enamel.

HAMMER MARKS

An even pattern of marks made by hammering metal over a steel stake with a planishing hammer. The resultant surface is visible through the fired transparent enamel.

INORGANIC

Applied to all substances that do not contain carbon as a constituent—metals, rocks, minerals, enamels, and a variety of earths.

KILN

A large oven, usually of brick construction, used for firing clay wares and pottery.

LACQUER

Clear and hard drying natural or artificial varnish applied with a brush to bare polished metal surfaces or edges of bowls and trays to preserve a shiny surface.

LAVENDER OIL

A type of oil used in finely ground enamels so that they may be painted on with a brush.

LEADBEARING

A term specifically applied to enamels in which lead oxide is used as one of the principal fluxes. Reduces the melting temperature.

LEADLESS

Any enamel which does not contain lead.

LUSTER

A pearly, thin coating of a metallic solution fused onto the enamel surface. Made from silver, gold or copper.

MELTING POINT

The temperature at which a solid changes into a liquid.

MESH

The numerous openings of a screen or sieve. A 200 mesh sieve has 200 openings to the square inch, an 80 mesh sieve has 80 openings to the square inch.

OILS

Any one of a variety of oils in which enamels are finely ground to make a paste suitable for silk screen application.

OPALESCENT ENAMELS

Enamels having a milky appearance; semi-opaque and transparent.

ORGANDY

A thin material similar to silk used for silk screening designs onto enamel surfaces.

OPAQUE

An enamel which is not transparent and does not show through to the metal underneath.

PAINTER'S ENAMEL

A transparent base, high lead enamel prepared by grinding in oil; available in all colors and tonal values.

PAPER

Any type of paper, absorbent or glossy, to be used for stencil cutting for the application of enamel to metal.

PICKLING

The practice of cleaning and treating metals, preparatory to applying the enamel, by dipping in a hot acid and water bath.

PLANISHING

Hammering metal over a steel stake; produces a hammer-marked surface.

PLATING

An electroplating process whereby one metal is coated with a thin layer of another metal—such as silver or aluminum-plated steel.

PLATINUM

A silver-gray metal soluble in aqua regia. Can be purchased in liquid, leaf or paste form. Used for decorating fired enamel surfaces.

PROPANE

A colorless gas for hand torches such as the Bernz-o-matic; used for jewelry and small enameling instead of a furnace.

PYROMETER

An instrument for measuring the degree of heat in an enameling furnace.

RESPIRATOR

A mask to cover the nose and mouth when working with acids, spraying lead enamels, etc.

ROUGE

A cake of red compound applied to a cloth buffer to put high polish on metals.

RUBBER SQUEEGEE

A narrow band of hard black rubber encased in a piece of wood used to force enamel paste through a silk screen stencil.

ROUND NOSED PLIERS

Pliers used for bending and twisting metal objects: animals, birds, jewelry, etc.

SGRAFFITO

An ancient pottery decorating technique in which a surface coating is scratched through to reveal the ground color underneath; adapted by the author for use in enameling. Effective for producing line drawings on enamel surfaces.

SLIP

Finely ground liquid enamel "slush," produced by grinding in a porcelain ball mill, using water and clay as suspending agents.

SLUSH

Same as "slip"; for dipping or spraying enamel onto metal or fired enamel surfaces. Water and clay used as suspending agents. Will produce crackle when fired over transparent surface.

SOLDER

A fusing metal or alloy used to unite under heat two or more metals. Silver solder (hard) is used for metals that are to be enameled in temperatures of 1400 or 1500°F. Soft solders cannot be used for enameling.

SPATULA

A thin metal blade with a handle for mixing enamel screening pastes on a slab or applying enamel to a fired enamel surface.

SPINNING

An operation in which a round disc of metal is forced to conform to a wooden chuck on a lathe with a manually operated steel tool.

SPOONING

Applying "slip" or "slush" enamel with a spoon or other small dispenser. Similar to slip trailing with rubber syringe applicator.

SPRAY GUN

A spray apparatus used with air compressor to apply enamel.

SQUEEGEE OIL

Oil used in grinding enamel for silk screen printing.

STAKE

Round, highly polished metal form upon which metals are hammered to produce an even, planished surface.

STEEL WOOL

Usually used with scouring powder and water to clean metal surfaces prior to enameling.

STENCIL

Sometimes called a "template," made of paper, plastic or silk; used for applying designs to enamel surfaces.

STENCIL BRUSH

A round-nosed bristle brush for pouncing enamel paste through a paper or plastic stencil.

STENCIL FRAME

Wooden frame used to hold silk for silk screen printing.

STENCIL KNIFE

A sharp blade with handle for cutting paper stencils.

STILTS

Small metal or fired clay pointed bars sometimes used to support enamel pieces in the furnace.

SULPHURIC ACID

Used to pickle copper or steel prior to enameling. The usual combination is one part acid and six parts water, usually in a warm state. (Always pour the acid into the water and not the water into the acid.)

TEMPLATE

A paper, plastic or metal stencil for easy application of designs to enamel surfaces.

114

THREAD

Thin or thick fired enamel drippings used for textural effects in enameling.

TIMER

A clock that can be set to ring a bell at the time designated for proper firing of enamels in the furnace.

TONGS

A laboratory appliance for holding hot objects, planches, and screens and for putting enamels in and out of the furnace.

TORCH

Propane hand torch (Bernz-o-matic) for fusing small enamels.

TRAGACANTH

A hard flake vegetable gum boiled in water and thinned for use as an enamel adhesive. Never used in a thick, heavy state.

TRIVET

A metal support made from chrome steel to hold enamel pieces while in the furnace. A non-scaling metal.

VITREOUS ENAMEL

A glass compounded to adhere successfully and fuse onto metals, producing a permanent bond. A specific enamel is made for each particular metal.

WET GRINDING

A combination of enamel frit, water, clay, and salts ground in a ball mill for three to four hours to produce "slush" or "slip." Used for dipping or spraying.

bibliography

Addison, Julia DeWolf. *Arts and Crafts in the Middle Ages.* Boston: L. C. Page & Co., 1908.

Andrews, A. I. *Enamels.* Champaign, Illinois: Garrard Press, 1936.

Bates, Kenneth F. *Enameling, Principles and Practice.* Cleveland: World Publishing Co., 1951.

Biegeleisen, J. I. and Max Arthur Cohn. *Silk Screen Techniques.* New York: Dover Publications, 1953.

Brown, W. N. *The Art of Enameling.* London: Scott, Greenwood and Co., 1900.

Bryant, Eugene E. *Porcelain Enameling Operations.* Cleveland, Enamelist Publishing Co., 1953.

Cleveland Museum of Art. *May Show Bulletin.* 1933.

Cunnynghame, H. H. *The Art of Enameling Metal.* Westminister: Archibald Constable & Co., Ltd., 1899.

De Koningh, H. *The Preparation of Precious and Other Metals for Enameling.* New York: The Norman W. Henley Publishing Co., 1930.

Feirer, John L. *Modern Metalcraft.* Peoria, Illinois: The Manual Arts Press, 1946.

Fisher, Alexander. *The Art of Enameling on Metal.* London: The Studio, 1906.

Hansen, J. E. *A Manual of Porcelain Enameling.* Cleveland: Enamelist Publishing Co., 1943.

Hart, G. F. and Golden Keeley. *Metal Work for Craftsmen.* London: Sir Isaac & Sons, Ltd., 1945.

Kosloff, Albert. *Screen Process Printing.* Cincinnati: Signs of the Times, 1956.

Landrum, R. D. *Enamels.* Cleveland: Harshaw Chemical Co., 1918.

Larom, Mary. *Enameling for Fun and Profit.* New York: David McKay Co., Inc., 1954.

Lehnert, Georg Hermann, ed. *Illustrierte Geschichte des Kunstgewerbeschule.* (Vol. I) Berlin: M. Oldenbourg, 1907.

Martin, Charles J. *How to Make Modern Jewelry.* New York: Simon and Schuster, 1949.

Millenet, L. E. and H. DeKoningh. *Enameling on Metal.* (Translated from the French by H. De-Koningh.) London: Crosby Lockwood and Sons, 1926.

Miller, John G. *Metal Art Crafts.* New York: D. Van Nostrand Company, 1948.

Morgan, J. Pierpont. *Catalogue of the Collections of Jewels and Precious Works of Art.* London: Chiswisk Press, 1910.

Neuburger, Albert. *The Technical Arts and Sciences of the Ancients.* New York: Macmillan Co., 1930.

Otten, Mizi and Kathe Berle. *The Art of Enameling Can Be Fun.* New York, 1950.

Pack, Greta. *Jewelry and Enameling.* New York: D. Van Nostrand, Inc., 1941.

Rosenthal, Rudolf and Helen L. Ratzka. *The Story of Modern Applied Art.* New York: Harper and Brothers, 1948.

Stuckert, L. *Die Emailfabrikation.* 1929.

Thompson, Thomas E. *Enameling on Copper and Other Metals.* Highland Park, Illinois: Thomas C. Thompson Co., 1950.

University of Pittsburgh, Department of Fine Arts. *History of Enamels.* Catalogue of Exhibition, April 8, 1950.

Untracht, Oppi. *Enameling on Metal.* New York: Greenberg Publishers, 1957.

Weaver, Robert A. *An Ancient Art becomes a Modern Industry.* Cleveland: Enamelist Publishing Co., 1934.

Wiener, Louis. *Hand Made Jewelry.* New York: D. Van Nostrand Co., 1948.

Winebrenner, D. Kenneth. *Jewelry Making as an Art Expression.* Scranton, Pa.: International Textbook Co., 1953.

Winter, Edward. *Porcelain Enamel Art for Beginners.* Cleveland: Enamelist Publishing Co., 1947.

Winter, Edward. *Enamel Art on Metals.* New York: Watson-Guptill Publications, Inc., 1958.

Zahn, Bert. *Screen Process Methods of Reproduction.* Chicago: Frederick J. Drake Co., 1958.

index